GCSE Edexcel Biology The Workbook

This book is for anyone doing **GCSE Edexcel Biology**.

It's full of **tricky questions**... each one designed to make you **sweat** — because that's the only way you'll get any **better**.

There are questions to see **what facts** you know. There are questions to see how well you can **apply those facts**. And there are questions to see what you know about **how science works**.

It's also got some daft bits in to try and make the whole experience at least vaguely entertaining for you.

What CGP is all about

Our sole aim here at CGP is to produce the highest quality books — carefully written, immaculately presented and dangerously close to being funny.

Then we work our socks off to get them out to you — at the cheapest possible prices.

Contents

Published by CGP

Editors:
Charlotte Burrows, Emma Elder, Mary Falkner, Ben Fletcher, Rosie McCurrie, Hayley Thompson.

Contributors:
Jane Davies, James Foster, Paddy Gannon, Dr Iona MJ Hamilton, Derek Harvey, Rebecca Harvey, Claire Ruthven, Adrian Schmit.

ISBN: 978 1 84762 607 3

With thanks to Helen Brace, Janet Cruse-Sawyer, Murray Hamilton, David Hickinson, and Edmund Robinson for the proofreading.
With thanks to Laura Jakubowski for the copyright research.

Graph on page 35 to show the number of cases of TB in the UK between 1997 and 2005 Source: The United Kingdom Parliament. Parliamentary material is reproduced with the permission of the Controller of HMSO on behalf of Parliament.

Graph to show the numbers of kidney transplant patients on page 99 and Table of Kidney Failure Statistics on page 114 reproduced with permission from the NHS UK Transplant. www.organdonation.nhs.uk

Every effort has been made to locate copyright holders and obtain permission to reproduce sources. For those sources where it has been difficult to trace the originator of the work, we would be grateful for information. If any copyright holder would like us to make an amendment to the acknowledgements, please notify us and we will gladly update the book at the next reprint. Thank you.

Printed by Elanders Ltd, Newcastle upon Tyne.
Clipart from Corel®
Based on the classic CGP style created by Richard Parsons.

Classification

Q1 Look at the list of **kingdoms** on the right and answer the questions below.

Protoctists
Prokaryotes
Fungi
Plants
Animals

a) Circle the kingdom that has no nucleus.

b) Give **one** reason why fungi are not placed in the plant kingdom.

....

c) Name **one** feature that protoctists have in common with prokaryotes.

....

d) Explain why viruses cannot be placed in any of the kingdoms listed above.

....

Q2 Organisms can be **classified** into kingdoms and then smaller groups, e.g. species.

a) Complete the subdivision of kingdoms using the words given below.

kingdom ⟶ phylum ⟶ .... ⟶ .... ⟶ .... ⟶ .... ⟶ species

genus order class family

b) For each of the following organisms, give **two** features that can be useful when classifying them.

i) Plants ....

ii) Animals ....

c) Describe the main characteristic of organisms in the phylum Chordata.

....

Q3 Animals can be classified as **vertebrates** or **invertebrates**. Vertebrates can be placed into one of five **classes** — fish, amphibians, reptiles, birds and mammals.

a) What is the main difference between vertebrates and invertebrates?

....

b) List **three** things that scientists take into account when dividing vertebrates into classes.

1. ....

2. ....

3. ....

c) Explain why some vertebrates, like the **duck-billed platypus**, aren't very easy to classify.

....

....

More on Classification

Q1 You are given a **sample** of a plant and an **identification key**.

1.	Does the plant have seeds?	Yes – go to 2. No – go to 3.
2.	Does the plant have flowers?	Yes – it is a flowering plant. No – go to 4.
3.	Does the plant have long stems with lots of small leaves?	Yes – it is a fern. No – go to 5.
4.	Does the plant produce cones?	Yes – it is a conifer. No – it is a grass.
5.	Does the plant have tiny leaves?	Yes – it is a moss. No – is it a fungus?

Use the key to identify the plant **from the sample** shown.

Type of plant: ....

Q2 The diagram on the right shows a **group of species** that live in **neighbouring** areas.

Western greenish warbler

Himalayan mountains

Two-barred warbler

Greenish warbler

Key: ←→ Interbreeds
■—■ Cannot interbreed

a) Which **two** species definitely cannot interbreed?

....

b) What is the name for a group of species like this?

....

Q3 Species are named using the **binomial system**.

a) What exactly does **binomial** mean?

....

b) Give **three** advantages of the binomial classification of organisms.

....

....

Q4 Explain why each of the following facts might make **accurate classification** of a species difficult.

a) Some plants reproduce **asexually**.

....

....

b) Many duck species **interbreed** to produce **fertile** offspring.

....

....

....

Variation

Q1 Complete this passage by circling the **best** word or phrase from each highlighted pair.

Usually, organisms of the same species **have differences / are identical.**
This is partly because different organisms have different **genes / cells**, which
they inherit from their parents. **Siblings / Identical twins** are exceptions to this.
But even these usually have some different features, such as **hair style / eye colour**,
and that is due to their **diet / environment**. The differences between individual
organisms are known as **variation / inheritance**.

Q2 For each of these characteristics, say whether it depends on **genes**, the **environment** or **both**.

a) A person's blood group. ....genes........

b) Someone being able to roll their tongue. ....enviroment........

c) Someone having cystic fibrosis. ....both........

d) Someone knowing how to speak Spanish. ....enviroment........

e) The colour of a plant's flowers. ....genes........

f) The height of a plant. ....both........

Q3 Helen and Stephanie are identical twins. Helen has dark hair and Stephanie is blonde.

a) Do you think that these are Helen and Stephanie's natural hair colours? Explain your answer.

No because as identical twins they have the same genes for hair colour.

b) Helen weighs 7 kg more than Stephanie. Say whether this is due to genes, environment or both, and explain your answer.

Both because one of them could have been born naturally larger ~~but~~ but also gained weight from enviromental factors.

c) Stephanie has a birthmark on her shoulder shaped like a monkey. Helen doesn't.
Do you think birthmarks are caused by your genes? Explain why.

No because not both of them have one even though they have the same genes

Top Tips: It's weird to think you only look the way you do because of your genes or your environment, or both. Apart from that dodgy haircut — you've only got yourself to blame for that.

Variation

Q4 Mr O'Riley breeds racehorses. He breeds his best black racing stallion, Snowball, with his best black racing mare, Goldie.

a) Why is there no guarantee that any foal born will be a champion racer?

b) Will the colour of the newborn foal be due to genes or to environment?

genes

Q5 Charlie did an experiment to examine the effect of **minerals** on the growth of **two species** of **wheat plant**. He took 60 seedlings of species 1, and divided them into six groups. He repeated this with species 2. He planted each group of seedlings in **identical pots of soil**, but gave them different concentrations of minerals. The table shows the results that Charlie got.

Concentration of mineral / ppm	Change in height of species 1 after 3 weeks / cm	Change in height of species 2 after 3 weeks / cm
0	0	0
100	2	12
200	6	21
300	15	29
400	17	34
500	21	40

a) Explain why Charlie used **ten** seedlings in each group, instead of just one.

To get more accurate results.

b) Charlie put all the seedlings into **identical pots** and used the **same type** of soil.

i) Explain why he did this.

So no other factors change the results.

ii) Suggest **two** other things that Charlie should try to keep the same.

The amount of water and light

c) What do Charlie's results suggest about the effect of minerals on the growth of these plants?

Minerals make the plants grow faster

d) Do you think that the growth of Charlie's plants was affected by genes, the environment or both? Explain your answer.

Both however as he tested his results on multiple seeds the enviroment will have affected his results more than their genes

Continuous and Discontinuous Variation

Q1 State whether there is **continuous** or **discontinuous** variation in each of these characteristics.

a) A person's blood group. ...discontinuous...

b) The distance between a person's pupils. ....

c) The colour of a courgette. ....

d) The height of a sunflower. ....

e) Antibiotic resistance. ....

Q2 Briefly describe a **practical** you could do to show **continuous** variation.

....

....

Q3 Greg measured **two** characteristics in a population of **pea plants**. The results are shown below.

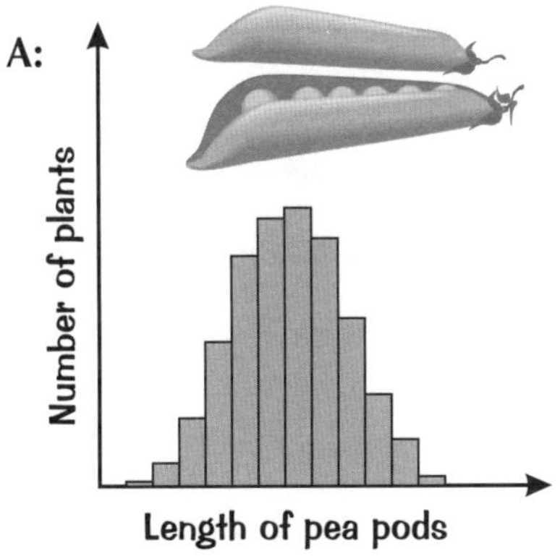

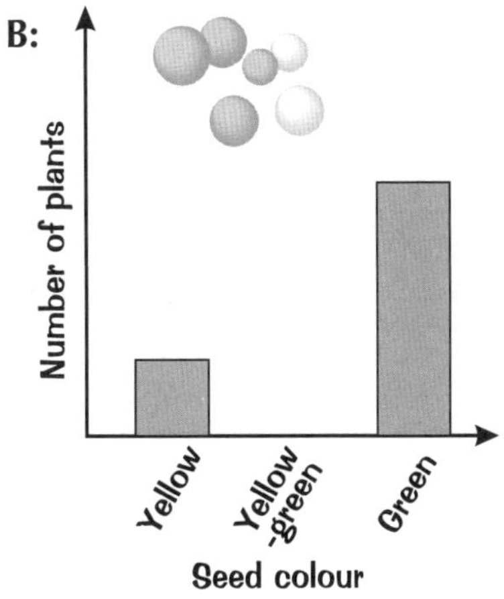

a) **i)** What does discontinuous variation mean?

....

....

ii) In which characteristic did Greg observe discontinuous variation? ....

b) **i)** What does continuous variation mean?

....

....

ii) In which characteristic did Greg observe continuous variation? ....

c) Which graph shows the shape of a normal distribution? ....

Extreme Environments

Q1 The picture below shows an **angler fish**. Angler fish live in very **deep seas**, where sunlight cannot penetrate.

Luminous organ that glows in the dark

Huge mouth with sharp teeth

a) What conditions make the deep sea a hostile environment?

....

....

b) Suggest how the luminous organ on its head helps the angler fish to stay alive in its environment.

....

c) Suggest how a huge mouth can help deep sea fish to stay alive in their environment.

....

Q2 There is usually a much higher density of life found on the seabed around **hydrothermal vents**.

a) Give **two** things that are provided by the vents that make it easier for life to exist around them.

....

b) The food webs around vents are not based on photosynthesis, unlike most others on Earth.

i) Name the process that hydrothermal vent food webs rely on.

....

ii) Briefly explain how this process works.

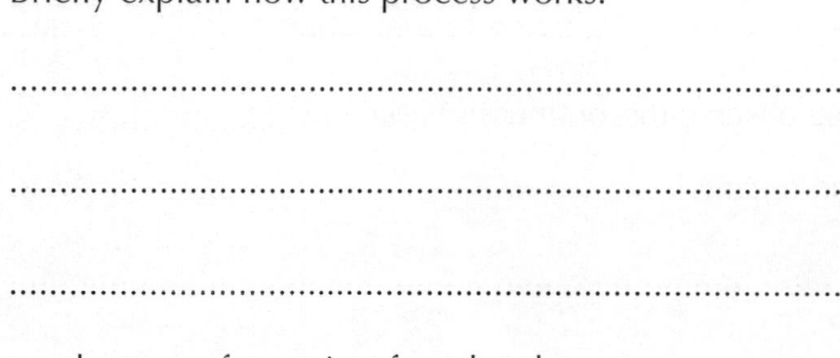

....

....

....

c) Name the type of organism found at the bottom of hydrothermal vent food webs.

....

Extreme Environments

Q3 Pictures of a **polar bear** and a small rodent called a **kangaroo rat** are shown below.

Diagrams are not to scale.

a) Which of these animals do you think has the smallest body surface area? ....

b) Which animal has the smallest body surface area **compared to its volume**? ....

Remember, long, thin shapes have a big surface area compared to their volume.

c) Explain how this animal's **shape** helps to reduce its body surface area compared to its volume.

....

d) Does having a **smaller** body surface area compared to volume mean that more or less **heat** can be lost from an animal's body?

....

e) The polar bear lives in the arctic. It has a **thick layer of blubber**, **large feet** and **greasy fur**. Explain how each of these adaptations helps the polar bear to survive.

....

....

....

....

Q4 Penguins living in the **Antarctic** have to survive very low temperatures. They have feathers, which trap air to form an **insulating layer**, and a thick layer of **fat** under their skin. The only places on their bodies that do not have a thick insulating layer are the feet and the flippers.

a) The muscles that operate a penguin's feet and flippers are not actually in these parts of its body, but in the main part of the body. Explain why this is important.

....

....

b) Penguins sometimes stand very close together in a group. Suggest how this behaviour might help them to survive.

....

Top Tips: Extreme environments are places with conditions that few species can cope with. For those that can, life's no picnic but on the plus side there's very little competition from other species.

Natural Selection and Evidence for Evolution

Q1 Explain what is meant by the term '**evolution**'.

....

....

Q2 The theory of evolution has been supported by **evidence** from **DNA research**.
Circle the correct word from the highlighted pair to complete the paragraph below.

Evolution suggests that all organisms have evolved from shared **common** / **distant** ancestors.
Closely related species diverged (evolved to become different species)
more recently / **a long time ago**. Evolution is caused by **rapid** / **gradual** changes in DNA.
Organisms that diverged away from each other recently should have **more** / **less** similar DNA.
Scientists have found that humans and chimps have **similar** / **different** DNA.

Q3 The theory of evolution by **natural selection** was developed by Charles Darwin.
Tick the sentences below that describe aspects of natural selection correctly.

- [ ] Genes don't vary enough within populations to make individuals look different.
- [ ] The best adapted animals and plants are most likely to survive.
- [ ] Some characteristics are passed on through reproduction from parent to offspring.
- [ ] Over time, there will be a higher proportion of individuals with poorly adapted characteristics compared to those with beneficial characteristics.
- [ ] Most organisms give birth to less young than can survive to adulthood.
- [ ] Individuals less well adapted to their environment are less likely to survive and reproduce.
- [ ] Populations increase rapidly in size, so organisms don't compete.

Q4 Explain how the emergence of **warfarin-resistant rats** supports the theory of evolution by natural selection.

....

....

....

Natural Selection and Evidence for Evolution

Q5 Describe **two** ways in which scientists validate new evidence.

1. ....

....

....

2. ....

....

....

Q6 The **peppered moth** is an insect that is often found on tree bark and is preyed on by birds. There are **two varieties** of peppered moth — a light form and a dark form. Until the 1850s, the **light form** was more common, but then the **dark form** became more widespread, particularly near cities.

Moths on tree bark in unpolluted area

Moths on tree bark in polluted area

a) Why do you think the lighter variety of the peppered moth was more common originally?

....

....

Hint: Use the diagrams to help you.

b) In the 1850s, the Industrial Revolution began — there was rapid growth in heavy industries in Britain. Why do you think the number of dark moths increased after this time?

....

....

c) Do you think a difference in genes or in environment would cause a dark moth to suddenly appear in a population of light moths? ....

Top Tips: Remember, evolution is a very gradual process — it doesn't just happen overnight. Make sure you really understand natural selection, so you can apply your knowledge to any question.

Speciation and Genes

Q1 Complete the passage using some of the words given below.

DNA	nucleus	genes	chromosomes	membrane	allele

Most cells in your body contain a structure called the ....

This structure contains strands of genetic information, packaged into ....

These strands are made of a chemical called ....

Sections of genetic material that control different characteristics are called ....

Q2 Write out these structures in order of size, **starting with the smallest**.

nucleus **gene** **chromosome** **cell**

1. .... 2. .... 3. .... 4. ....

Q3 a) Which of the following is the correct definition of the term '**alleles**'? Underline your choice.

'Alleles' is the collective term for all the genes found on a pair of chromosomes.

'Alleles' are different forms of the same gene.

'Alleles' are identical organisms produced by asexual reproduction.

b) Look at the two statements below and circle the one that is **true**.

Alleles give different versions of a characteristic.

All alleles give identical versions of a characteristic.

Q4 Isolation and natural selection can lead to **speciation**.

a) What is meant by the term '**isolation**'?

....

b) The diagrams below show the stages of speciation.
Draw lines to match the labels to the correct diagrams.

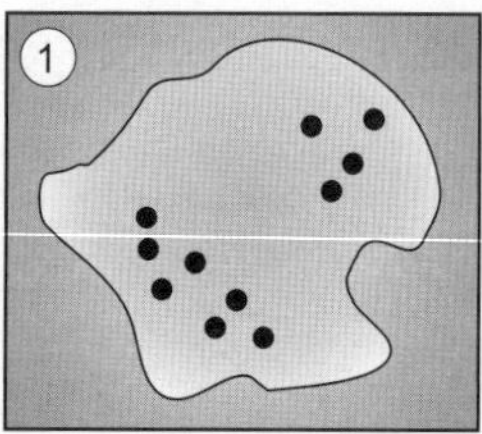

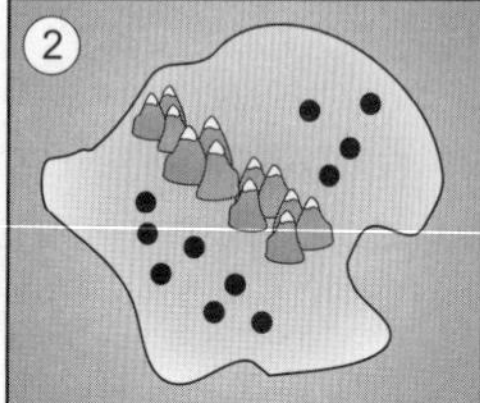

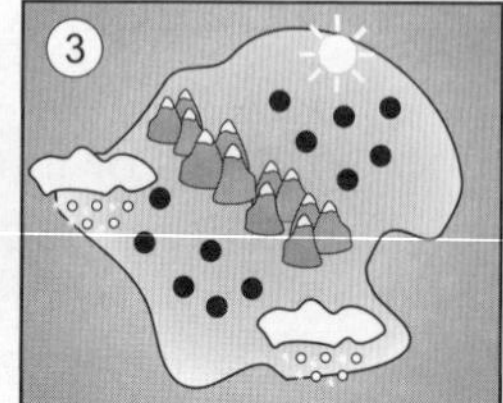

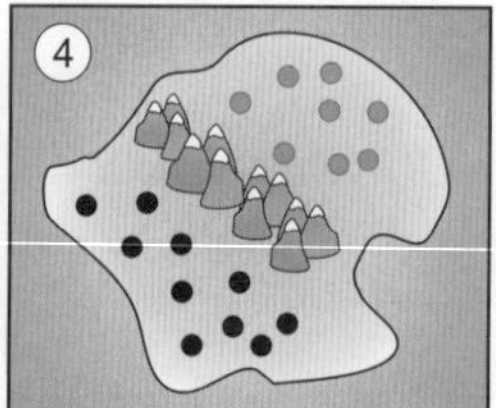

A new species develops.

The populations adapt to new environments.

There are two populations of the same species.

Physical barriers separate the populations.

Genetic Diagrams

Q1 Match each of the terms below with its meaning.

dominant	having two different alleles for a gene
genotype	having two identical alleles for a gene
heterozygous	shown in organisms heterozygous for that trait
homozygous	not shown in organisms heterozygous for that trait
phenotype	the actual characteristics of an individual
recessive	the alleles that an individual contains

Q2 Wilma carries a **recessive** allele for **red** hair and a **dominant** allele for **brown** hair.

a) What is Wilma's natural hair colour?

....

b) Is Wilma homozygous or heterozygous for this characteristic?

....

Q3 Fruit flies usually have **red** eyes. However, there are a small number of white-eyed fruit flies. Having **white** eyes is a **recessive** characteristic.

a) Complete the following sentences with either '**red eyes**' or '**white eyes**'.

i) **R** is the allele for ....

ii) **r** is the allele for ....

iii) Fruit flies with alleles **RR** or **Rr** will have ....

iv) Fruit flies with the alleles **rr** will have ....

b) Two fruit flies have the alleles **Rr**. They fall in love and get it on.

i) Complete this genetic diagram to show the possible offspring. One's been done for you.

parent's alleles ↓ / parent's alleles →	R	r
R	RR	
r		

Read down and across to work out what combination of alleles should be in each box.

ii) What is the probability that the fruit flies' offspring will have **white eyes**?

....

iii) The fruit flies have 16 offspring. How many of the offspring are **likely** to have **red eyes**?

....

Genetic Diagrams

Q4 The **seeds** of pea plants can be **smooth** or **wrinkled**. The allele for smooth seeds (**S**) is dominant. The allele for wrinkled seeds (**s**) is recessive.

a) Complete the genetic diagram below. It shows a cross between a homozygous smooth seed pea plant (genotype **SS**) and a homozygous wrinkled seed pea plant (genotype **ss**).

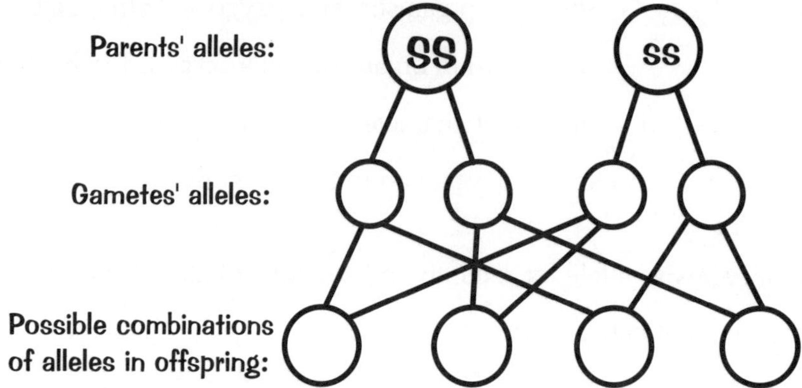

b) In this cross, what is the probability that any one of the offspring will have wrinkled seeds? Tick the correct box.

- ☐ 100% chance of being wrinkled.
- ☐ 50% chance of being wrinkled.
- ☐ 25% chance of being wrinkled.
- ☐ 0% chance of being wrinkled.

Pictures of peas are very dull. So here's a picture of a tapir instead.

c) Complete the genetic diagram below to show the possible combinations of alleles in the offspring.

parent's alleles		parent's alleles: S	parent's alleles: s
	S		
	s		

d) Mrs Maguire crosses two pea plants with the alleles Ss. Is the following statement **true** or **false**? Tick the correct box.

"If Mrs Maguire gets 12 new seedlings as a result of her cross, the most likely number of seedlings with wrinkled seeds will be 3."

True ☐ False ☐

Top Tip: Lots of people prefer the grid-type genetic diagrams, but don't be scared of the ones with the blobs and lines. They look like a crazy mess at first but they're actually dead simple — every one of the four offspring circles must have **one letter** from **each** parent, **never** two from the same parent.

Genetic Diagrams and Disorders

Q1 **Sickle-cell anaemia** is a **recessive genetic disorder** which affects the **red blood cells**. The recessive allele for sickle-cell anaemia is **a**, and the dominant allele is **A**.

a) Give **two symptoms** of sickle-cell anaemia.

1. .... 2. ....

b) What combination of alleles is possessed by:

i) a carrier for sickle-cell anaemia. ....

ii) a sufferer of sickle-cell anaemia. ....

iii) an unaffected person (who is not a carrier). ....

Q2 a) What is cystic fibrosis? Choose from the words below to fill in the gaps.

allele carrier genetic parents lung recessive pancreas mucus breathing

Cystic fibrosis is a .... disorder. It is inherited from the .... The disease is .... That means a person must have two copies of the faulty .... Cystic fibrosis results in the body producing a lot of thick, sticky .... in the air passages, gut and .... Symptoms include difficulty .... and .... infections. A person with one copy of the recessive allele is a ....

b) Complete the following genetic diagram showing the inheritance of cystic fibrosis.

Parents: Ff Ff

Gametes:

Offspring:

c) **i)** In the above genetic diagram, what would be the expected **ratio** of children without cystic fibrosis : children with cystic fibrosis?

....

ii) In the above genetic diagram, what is the probability of a child being a **carrier** of the cystic fibrosis allele (but not having the disease)?

....

Genetic Diagrams and Disorders

Q3 The family tree below shows a family with a history of **cystic fibrosis**. Both Libby and Anne are pregnant. They know the sexes of their babies but not whether they have the disorder.

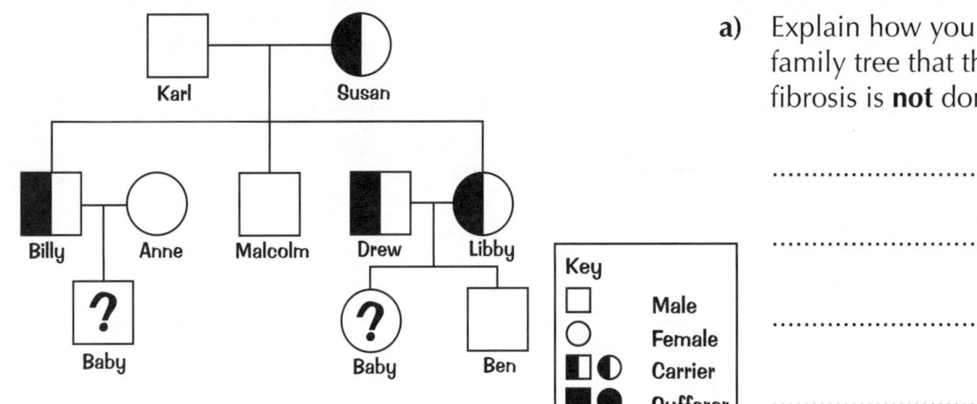

a) Explain how you can tell from the family tree that the allele for cystic fibrosis is **not** dominant.

....

....

....

....

b) i) Complete the table to show the percentage chances of Libby's and Anne's babies being carriers and sufferers.

Sketch a genetic diagram if it helps.

	Carrier	Sufferer
Libby		
Anne		

ii) From the information in part **i)** which mother, Libby or Anne, might decide to have their baby screened for cystic fibrosis?

....

Q4 The **genetic pedigree diagram** below shows the inheritance of **sickle cell anaemia** in one family.

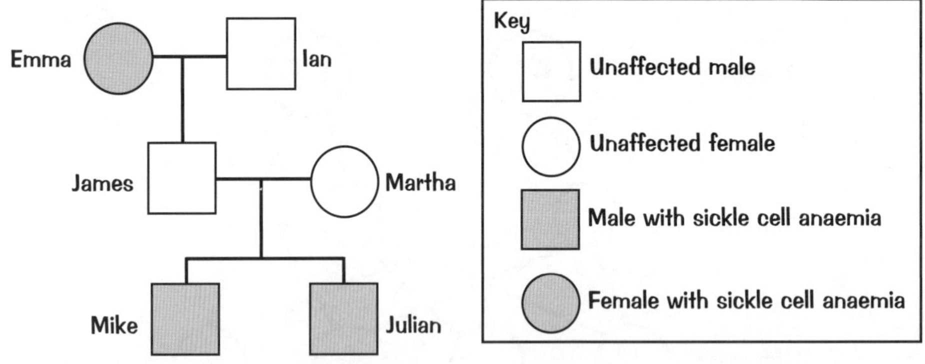

a) Name one female who is **homozygous** for the sickle cell anaemia allele. ....

b) Name one female who is a **carrier** for sickle cell anaemia. ....

c) If James and Martha have another child, what is the chance it will have sickle cell anaemia?

....

Write the genotypes you know on the diagram — this'll help you to work out the ones you don't know.

Top Tip: Pedigree diagrams aren't as scary as they look, just work through them slowly. And remember — with recessive disorders affected individuals are always homozygous, so any children they have will always have at least one recessive allele.

Mixed Questions — B1 Topic 1

Q1 Two types of **goose** found in the UK are the greylag goose and the white-fronted goose. The Latin name for the greylag goose is ***Anser anser*** and the white-fronted goose is ***Anser albifrons***.

a) How can you tell that these two geese are different species?

....

b) How can you tell that the two species must be closely related?

....

c) What name is given to the system of identifying species by giving them two names?

....

d) Give a definition for the term '**species**'.

....

e) **i)** What **kingdom** do geese belong to?

....

ii) Give one feature of this kingdom.

....

Q2 The **Arctic fox** is adapted for Arctic conditions. For example, it has thick white fur.

a) Explain why thick white fur is useful in Arctic conditions.

....

....

b) Briefly explain how **natural selection** has led to adaptations such as these becoming widespread in the Arctic fox population.

....

....

....

c) A different species of fox moves to the Arctic. Suggest what effect this may have on the population of Arctic foxes currently living there, and explain why.

....

....

Mixed Questions — B1 Topic 1

Q3 In the Galapagos Islands, different varieties of **giant tortoise** are found on different islands. For example, where the main available food is grass, the tortoises have a dome-shaped shell. However, where the main food is tall cacti, the tortoises have a saddle-backed shell, which allows them to raise their heads higher to feed.

dome-shelled tortoise

saddle-back tortoise

a) Give one example of how the tortoises vary.

....

b) Other than the environment, what causes variation?

....

c) Explain how variation within a species can make accurate classification difficult.

....

d) Different tortoises weigh different amounts.

i) Is the weight of a tortoise affected by its environment? Explain your answer.

....

....

ii) Is weight an example of continuous or discontinuous variation? Explain your answer.

....

....

Q4 Mr and Mrs Carlton are both carriers of **cystic fibrosis** (CF), a **recessive** genetic disorder. The symbol '**c**' is used to represent the recessive allele.

a) What is an allele?

....

....

male gametes

female gametes

b) Mr and Mrs Carlton are planning a family.
Complete the genetic diagram to show the probability of one of their children suffering from the disorder.
Use the symbols **C** and **c** to represent the alleles.

c) What is the probability of the child being a CF sufferer? ....

Homeostasis

Q1 Homeostasis is an important process in the human body.

a) Define **homeostasis**.

....

b) Give **two** examples of conditions in the body that are controlled by homeostasis.

1. .... 2. ....

Q2 Complete the following passage by choosing the correct words from those provided.

cold	hairs	nerve	erector	air	warm	fat	muscle

Your skin has lots of .... endings in it that act as temperature receptors. When they detect that you are too ...., the .... muscles in the dermis contract. This makes the .... on your skin stand on end. They trap an insulating layer of ...., which keeps you warm.

Q3 Tim goes outside on a hot day. The sentences below explain how **negative feedback** acts to keep his body temperature constant. Number the sentences to show the correct order.

- [ ] **His brain detects an increase in body temperature.**
- [ ] **Tim's body temperature drops to a normal level.**
- [1] **Tim's body temperature begins to rise.**
- [ ] **It triggers a series of responses that make Tim's body temperature fall.**

The first one has been done for you.

Q4 Your body has various techniques for adjusting body temperature to keep it constant.

a) Name the part of the brain that controls body temperature. ....

b) Explain how **sweating** helps to lower your body temperature.

....

....

c) i) Explain what vasodilation and vasoconstriction are.

....

....

ii) How do vasodilation and vasoconstriction help to keep your body temperature constant?

....

....

Hormones and Nerves

Q1 Complete the following passage by choosing the correct words from those given.

blood fast long target short chemicals air slow endocrine impulses nerve

Hormones are .... which are made in .... glands and released into the .... They are carried around the body until they reach a .... organ where they act. Hormones are generally quite .... to act, but their effects last a .... time.

Q2 Give two differences between responses due to **hormones** and those due to the **nervous system**.

1. ....

2. ....

Q3 Hormones can reach **every cell** in the body. Explain why only the **target cells** respond to the hormone while the others are unaffected.

....

....

Q4 **Neurones** transmit electrical impulses around the body. A diagram of a neurone is shown below.

a) Match the labels to the parts of the neurone by putting the correct letters in the boxes.

A synapse B nucleus D axon

C myelin sheath E dendrons

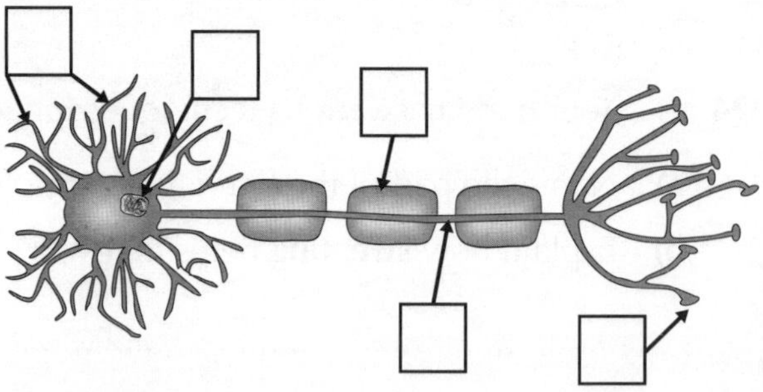

b) Briefly explain the function of:

i) the **dendrons** ....

ii) the **myelin sheath** ....

....

c) Describe the role of **neurotransmitters** in transmitting a nerve impulse.

....

....

The Nervous System

Q1 Decide whether the following statements are **true** or **false**.

		True	False
a)	Muscles and glands are both effectors.	☐	☐
b)	Muscles contract in response to electrical signals.	☐	☐
c)	Glands secrete substances in response to a nervous impulse.	☐	☐
d)	Hormones are secreted by nerves.	☐	☐

Q2 Complete the following passage by choosing the correct words from the box.

brain	central	motor	effectors	spinal	electrical	sensory

The .... nervous system refers to all neurones found in the .... and .... cord. Neurones transmit .... impulses from sense organs to the CNS along .... neurones. Impulses from the CNS are sent along .... neurones to ....

Q3 Circle the correct word(s) from each pair to complete these sentences about **neurones**.

a) Sensory neurones have **long** / **short** dendrons and **long** / **short** axons.

b) Relay neurones have many **long** / **short** dendrons and **long** / **short** axons.
They carry nerve impulses from **sensory** / **motor** neurones to **sensory** / **motor** neurones.

c) Motor neurones have many short dendrons and **many short axons** / **one long axon**.

Q4 Complete the table with the entries given to show the **sense organs** and the type of **receptors** they contain.

Sense organ	Receptor type
	Light
Nose	
	Sound / balance
Tongue	
	Touch / temperature

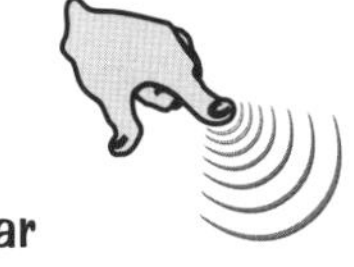

Ear

Taste

Skin

Smell

Eye

The Nervous System

Q5 Give **two** reasons why it is important for animals to be able to **detect changes** in their surroundings.

....

....

Q6 Explain why a man with a **damaged spinal cord** may not be able to feel someone touching his toe.

....

....

....

Q7 The nervous system is made up of several different parts.

a) Draw arrows between the boxes in the diagram to show the flow of information from a stimulus through the nervous system to the response.

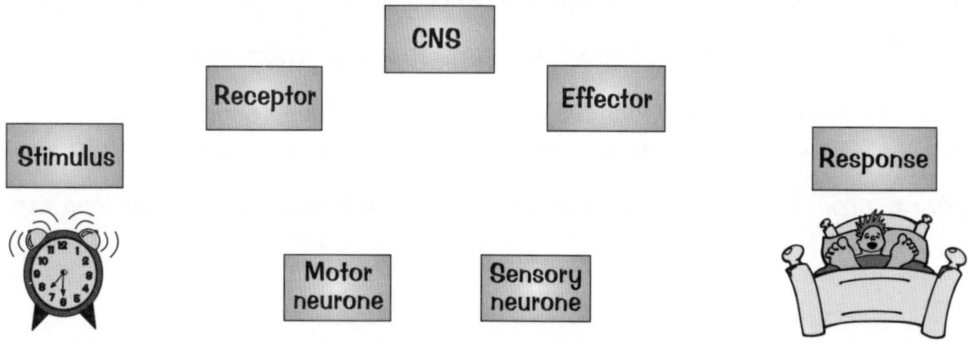

CNS

Receptor

Effector

Stimulus

Response

Motor neurone

Sensory neurone

b) Outline the function of the following parts of the nervous system:

i) Receptor cells ....

ii) Sensory neurones ....

iii) CNS ....

iv) Motor neurones ....

v) Effector cells ....

c) The sensory system is driven by stimuli. What is a stimulus?

....

Investigating Stimuli and Reflexes

Q1 Circle the correct answers to complete the following sentences.

a) Reflexes happen more **quickly** / **slowly** than considered responses.

b) The **vertebrae** / **spinal cord** can coordinate a reflex response.

c) The main purpose of a reflex is to **protect** / **display** the body.

d) Reflexes happen **with** / **without** conscious thought.

Q2 When you touch something hot with a finger you **automatically** pull the finger away. The diagram shows some parts of the nervous system involved in this **reflex action**.

receptor in skin

X

Y

muscle

Z

spinal cord

What type of neurone is:

a) neurone **X**? ....

b) neurone **Y**? ....

c) neurone **Z**? ....

Q3 Explain why a **reflex** reaction is faster than a **voluntary** reaction.

Think about where the impulse has to go to.

....

....

....

Q4 Explain what a **reflex arc** is.

....

....

....

Top Tips: Reflexes are really fast — that's the whole point of them. And the fewer synapses the signals have to cross, the faster the reaction. Doctors test people's reflexes by tapping below their knees to make their legs jerk. This reflex takes less than 50 milliseconds as only one synapse is involved.

Investigating Stimuli and Reflexes

Q5 Read the passage below and then answer the questions.

'Ducking' when an object flies at your head is an example of a reflex action. The eyes detect an object approaching at speed and send a signal to the brain. The brain immediately sends a signal back out to the various muscles that need to contract in order to move the head out of the way.

a) What sort of neurone carries the signal from the eyes to the brain? ....

b) From the passage, identify the following:

i) The stimulus .... **ii)** The receptor ....

iii) The effectors .... **iv)** The response ....

Q6 John and Marc investigated how **sensitive** different parts of the body are to **pressure**. They stuck two pins in a cork 0.5 cm apart. The pins were placed on different parts of the body. Ten pupils took part — they were blindfolded and reported "yes" or "no" to feeling both points. The results of the experiment are shown in the table.

Area of the body tested	Number of pupils reporting 'yes'
Sole of foot	2
Knee	3
Fingertip	10
Back of hand	5
Lip	9

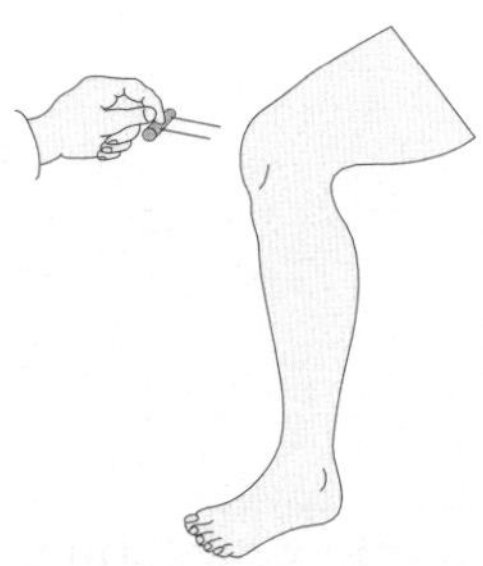

a) Which part of the body do the results suggest is:

i) most sensitive? .... **ii)** least sensitive? ....

b) From the results above, which part of the body do you think contains the greatest concentration of **pressure receptors**? Explain your answer.

....

....

c) John and Marc took it in turns to test the pupils. Their teacher suggested that if only one of the boys had done all the testing, the experiment would have been fairer. Explain why.

....

....

d) Each pupil was tested once. Suggest how you might make the test more reliable.

....

....

Insulin and Diabetes

Q1 Most people's **blood sugar** level is controlled as part of **homeostasis**.

a) Where does the **sugar** in your blood come from?

....

b) Name the **two** main **organs** that are involved in the control of blood sugar levels.

....

c) Name **two hormones** involved in the regulation of blood sugar level.

....

Q2 Complete the flow chart to show what happens when the **glucose** level in the blood gets too **high**.

Blood contains too much glucose.

↘

.... is released by the ....

↘

.... makes the .... store glucose.
Excess blood glucose is converted to ....

↘

.... is removed from the ....

↘

Blood glucose level is now ....
So .... stops being released.

Q3 Explain how the blood sugar level is controlled when there is **not enough** glucose in the blood.

....

....

....

Insulin and Diabetes

Q4 Approximately **2.6 million** people in the UK have **diabetes**.

a) Explain what **type 1** diabetes is.

....

b) **i)** Choose the correct word to complete the following sentence:

> People with type 1 diabetes can control their blood glucose by injecting insulin into the **subcutaneous fat** / **pancreas**.

ii) How does taking regular exercise affect the amount of insulin a person needs to inject?

....

c) Explain what **type 2** diabetes is.

....

....

d) Give **two** ways in which type 2 diabetes can be controlled.

1. ....

2. ....

e) What is the link between type 2 diabetes and obesity?

....

Q5 Bob has a height of 1.85 m and a mass of 100 kg.
Jim has a height of 175 cm and a mass of 95 kg.

Make sure you use kg and m in your calculations.

a) Calculate the BMI of:

i) Bob ....

....

ii) Jim ....

....

b) Who would be classified as obese: Jim, Bob, neither or both? Explain your answer.

....

Top Tips: Although diabetes is a serious disease, many diabetics are able to control their blood sugar level and carry on with normal lives. Sir Steve Redgrave even won a gold medal at the Olympics after he had been diagnosed with type 1 diabetes.

Plant Growth Hormones

Q1 Decide whether the following statements are **true** or **false**.

		True	False
a)	Plant shoots grow away from light.	☐	☐
b)	Plant roots grow in the same direction that gravity acts.	☐	☐
c)	If the tip of a shoot is removed, the shoot may stop growing upwards.	☐	☐
d)	Gibberellin affects seed germination and flowering.	☐	☐

Q2 Some potted plants are growing in a shed lit only by **electric lights**. Circle the letters above the lights that have **broken**.

A B C D E

Q3 Draw lines to match the two phrases below with their correct **definition** from underneath.

Positive phototropism | Positive gravitropism

Growing towards water | Growing upwards | Growing towards light | Growing downwards

Q4 Choose the correct word from each pair to complete the following paragraph.

When a shoot tip is exposed to light from one side, auxin accumulates on the side that's in the **light** / **shade**. This makes the cells elongate **faster** / **slower** on the shaded side, so the shoot bends **away from** / **towards** the light. In roots, auxin accumulates on the **upper** / **lower** side. This makes the cells elongate **faster** / **slower** on the upper side, so the root bends **downwards** / **upwards**.

Q5 **Auxin** affects plant shoots and roots differently.

a) Describe the **difference** between how auxin affects cells in the shoots and in the roots of plants.

....

....

b) Some side roots of plants grow at an angle to the main root, instead of straight down under the influence of gravity. Suggest why this might be an **advantage** for the plant.

....

Plant Growth Hormones — Experiments

Q1 Some students watered **four seeds** with four **different solutions** for one month. The table below shows their results.

Solution	Plant height (cm)
Water	19
Water + auxin	27
Water + gibberellin	25
Water + auxin + gibberellin	33

a) Describe what the results show.

....

....

b) Suggest what the students should do to increase the **reliability** of their results.

....

....

Q2 Vicky used three seedlings to investigate plant growth. Each seedling was prepared differently (see table). All three were placed in the same conditions, exposed to light from **one** direction and left for five hours. She recorded her results in the table below.

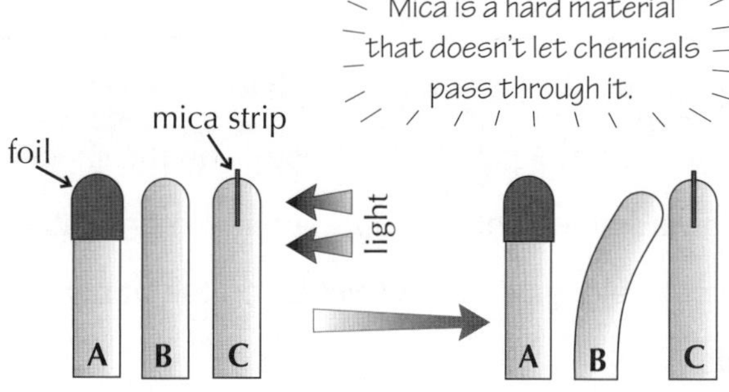

Seedling	Preparation	Observation after 5 hours
A	foil covering tip	no change
B	left alone	tip bent towards the light
C	mica strip through centre of tip	no change

a) Suggest why seedling A and seedling C failed to respond to the light.

Seedling A ....

....

Seedling C ....

....

b) Suggest how the experiment could be improved.

....

Commercial Use of Plant Hormones

Q1 Describe four ways in which **plant hormones** can be used **commercially**.

1. ....

2. ....

3. ....

4. ....

Q2 Ronald owns a fruit farm which grows satsumas. The fruit is picked before it is ripe and transported to market.

fruit picked → fruit packaged → fruit transported to market → fruit displayed

a) Suggest why the satsumas are picked before they are ripe.

....

....

b) i) How could the unripened satsumas be ripened in time to reach the market?

....

ii) At what stage in the diagram above should the satsumas be ripened?

....

Q3 Sanjay owns two neighbouring fields — **Field A** and **Field B**. They are an identical size, have the same soil and he uses the same fertiliser regime for both. The only difference is that he applies a weedkiller containing plant growth hormones to Field B but not Field A.

This table shows the yields for both fields.

Year	1997	1998	1999	2000	2001
Barley yield from field A, kg/ha	35	28	33	37	34
Barley yield from field B, kg/ha	48	39	44	49	43

a) What effect did the weedkiller have on crop yield?

....

b) Explain how this type of weedkiller works.

....

....

Mixed Questions — B1 Topic 2

Q1 **Reflex actions** are **automatic responses** to a stimulus.

a) Give one advantage of reflex actions to the body.

....

b) Which part of the nervous system is used to coordinate a reflex response?

....

c) Below are two situations which would cause reflex actions.

A: Stepping on a drawing pin with bare feet.
B: Smelling food when hungry.

Complete the table below for each of the examples given above.

Saliva production often increases when you smell food.

	A	B
stimulus		
receptor		
effector		
response		

Q2 **Hormones** and **neurones** pass signals around the body.

a) Hormones can affect different parts of the body at the same time. Explain how.

....

....

b) Are the effects of hormones **long-lasting** or **short-lasting** compared to the effect of nerves?

....

c) Where nerves are joined together, chemicals transmit the message between them.

i) What is the name for this **connection** between nerves?

....

ii) What is the name of the **type of chemical** that transmits messages between nerve endings?

....

d) Give the name for a pathway of neurones that goes from stimulus to response **without** passing through the conscious part of the brain.

....

Mixed Questions — B1 Topic 2

Q3 The diagram below shows how blood sugar level is controlled in humans.

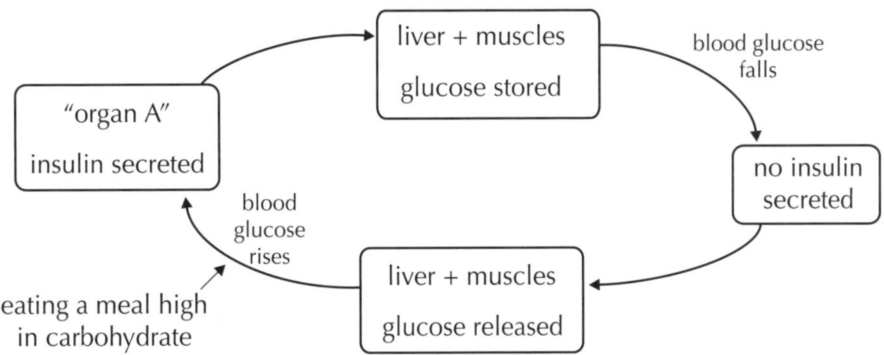

a) Name "organ A" in the diagram above.

....

b) Excess glucose is removed from your blood and stored in the liver and muscles.

i) Which hormone brings about the removal of glucose?

....

ii) Some people have diabetes (type 1) and cannot produce this hormone.
Briefly describe **one** way that diabetes is **controlled**.

....

Q4 A farmer watered 100 poppy plants and 100 wheat plants. He watered 50 of each plant species with a solution containing a **growth hormone**, and the other 50 just with **water**. The results are shown in the table below.

Plant species	Average height without growth hormone	Average height with growth hormone
Poppy (a broad-leaved weed)	65.8 cm	89.2 cm
Wheat (a narrow-leaved crop)	70.3 cm	70.2 cm

a) Describe the results shown in the table.

....

b) Suggest a potential use of large doses of the growth hormone for wheat farmers.

....

c) Name a plant hormone that could produce the results seen in poppies.

....

Drugs

Q1 a) What is a drug?

....

....

b) What does the term physical addiction mean?

....

....

c) Some drugs cause the body to develop a tolerance to them. What does this mean?

....

....

Q2 a) **Complete** the table below, which shows different types of drug and their effects on the body.

Type of drug	Example	Effects
Depressants		
	Morphine	Decrease the feeling of pain
Stimulants		
		Distort what is seen and heard

b) Briefly describe how morphine decreases the feeling of pain.

....

Q3 Different drugs have different effects on the nervous system.

a) Why is it dangerous to drive or operate machinery when under the influence of a depressant?

....

....

b) Caffeine is a legal drug in the UK. Why isn't it dangerous to drive under the influence of this drug?

....

....

Drugs

Q4 Tom and Jane did an experiment on **reaction times**. Tom held a ruler vertically between Jane's thumb and forefinger, with her forefinger in line with the zero mark. Tom dropped the ruler **without warning** and measured how far it fell before Jane caught it. They repeated their experiment three times. The three measurements (**in cm**) were **15**, **28** and **8**.

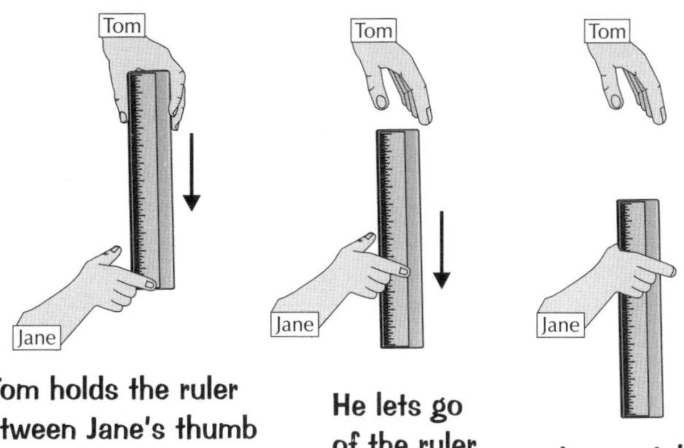

a) Suggest two reasons why the results varied so much.

1. ....

2. ....

b) Tom and Jane's teacher said that they needed to repeat their experiment at least 10 times. Why did she suggest so many repeats?

....

....

Tom and Jane tested the effect of **caffeine** on reaction times. They each drank one cup of coffee — either **regular** coffee or **decaffeinated** coffee. Then they repeated the above experiment 10 times.

c) Tom and Jane made sure neither of them knew which cup of coffee they had. Why do you think they did this?

....

....

....

d) Their results are shown in the table on the right.

i) Complete the table.

ii) Who do you think drank the regular coffee?

....

	Distance before coffee (cm)		Distance after coffee (cm)	
Trial	Tom	Jane	Tom	Jane
1	16	12	22	15
2	27	17	28	9
3	9	8	15	16
4	14	19	7	12
5	11	24	16	21
6	26	21	9	7
7	29	16	24	12
8	18	19	18	17
9	11	6	16	8
10	19	16	20	14
Mean	18			

Smoking, Alcohol and Organ Transplants

Q1 Alcohol has a number of **short-term effects**. State the effects it has on:

a) A person's behaviour.

....

b) A person's vision.

....

c) A person's reactions.

....

Q2 Complete the passage below by choosing the correct words from those given.

harmless long-term cleaning brain cirrhosis death damage liver poisonous blood

As well as affecting a person straight away, alcohol has .... effects, which means it affects a person in the future. Alcohol is .... Normally, the .... breaks down the toxic alcohol into .... by-products. But drinking too much too often causes the .... of liver cells, forming scar tissue that starts to block .... flow through the liver — this is called .... If the liver can't do its normal job of .... the blood, dangerous substances start to build up and .... the rest of the body. Too much drinking can also lead to .... damage.

Q3 Smoking tobacco can cause many different **health problems**, including cancer.
However, the habit is still widespread, mainly because smokers find it **difficult to stop**.

a) Explain why people find it difficult to stop smoking.

....

b) Pregnant women are strongly advised not to smoke.
What effect can smoking have on a baby's birth weight?

....

c) Explain how smoking whilst pregnant can cause this problem.

....

....

Top Tips: Tobacco and alcohol are totally legal substances but they're potentially dangerous drugs too. Alcohol is dangerous if used to excess and cigarettes are just full of poisonous chemicals.

Smoking, Alcohol and Organ Transplants

Q4 Many people wish to **donate organs** after they die so that other people can benefit.

a) What can a person do to officially state their wish to donate their organs?

....

b) Who can **object** to the removal of the donor's organs?

....

c) A patient who had liver cirrhosis after drinking too much alcohol was given a liver transplant.

i) Give a reason **in support** of this operation.

....

ii) Give **one** possible reason why some people would be **against** this operation.

....

d) What might a clinically obese person be asked to do before being considered for a heart transplant?

....

Q5 The graph shows how the number of **smokers** aged between 35 and 54 in the UK has changed since 1950.

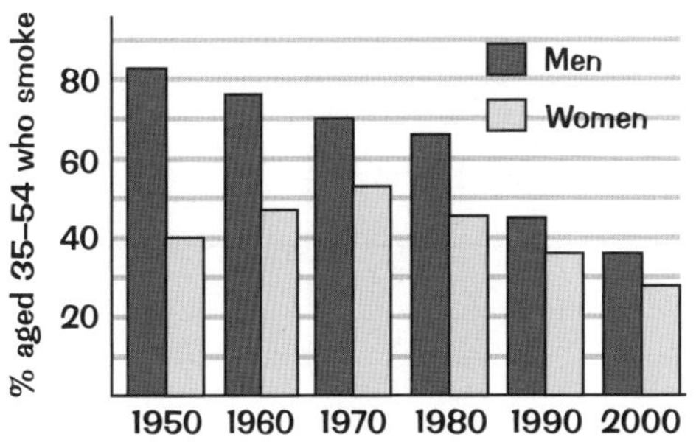

a) What percentage of **men** smoked in 1970?

....

b) Describe the main **trends** you can see in this graph.

....

....

....

....

c) Why are smokers more likely to suffer from **cancers**?

....

....

Infectious Diseases

Q1 Decide whether the following statements are **true** or **false**.

		True	False
a)	Infectious diseases are caused by pathogens.	☐	☐
b)	Infectious diseases can be passed on genetically.	☐	☐
c)	All pathogens are bacteria.	☐	☐
d)	Living organisms do not cause infectious diseases.	☐	☐

Q2 Complete the following passage by circling the correct words.

Influenza is caused by a **virus / bacterium**. It is spread by **vectors / droplets in air** — in the same way as **colds / Salmonella**. It's transmitted when an infected person coughs or sneezes near someone. People with symptoms should **stay at home / go to work** and use tissues when they sneeze.

HIV is a **virus / bacterium** that causes **Salmonella / AIDS**. It is passed on via **contact / body fluids**.

Q3 Complete the table below about the different ways in which organisms transmit diseases.

Disease	Cholera	Salmonella		Athlete's foot
Type of organism	bacterium			
How it is transmitted			by the *Anopheles* mosquito	

Q4 Dysentery is a disease that is spread by a **vector**.

a) Name a vector that carries dysentery.

....

b) How does this vector spread dysentery?

....

Infectious Diseases

Q5 The graph shows the change in someone's **body temperature** during a **flu infection**. Their temperature was recorded at the same time every day.

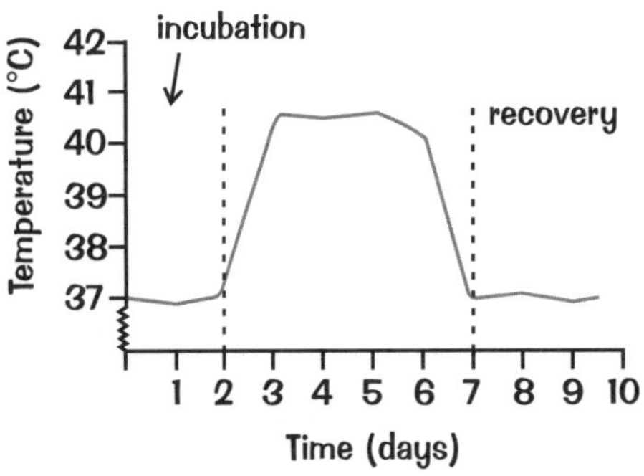

a) What was the maximum body temperature during this illness?

....

b) Approximately how many days after direct contact with someone infected with flu might you start to feel unwell?

....

Q6 The body has several methods of **defending itself** against the entry of **pathogens**. Below are some examples of how some bacterial pathogens can **enter the body**. In each case, describe how your body **prevents** against **illness**.

a) *Staphylococcus aureus* can cause blood poisoning by getting into the blood through cuts.

....

b) *Streptococcus pneumoniae* can enter the body from the air as a person breathes.

....

Q7 Give **two** examples of **chemical barriers** and explain the role each plays in defending the body.

1. ....

....

2. ....

....

Q8 TB is a bacterial infection that is spread by droplets in air. The graph shows the variation in the number of cases of **TB** in the **UK** between 1997 and 2005.

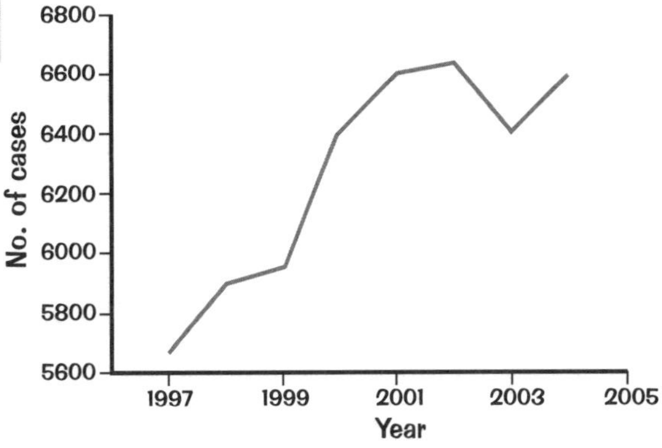

a) **i)** How many cases were there in 1998?

....

ii) In which year was the number of cases 6400?

....

b) Describe the **general trend** shown by the graph.

....

More About Drugs

Q1 Complete the following passage by circling the correct words.

Antibiotics are **drugs / antiseptics** used **inside / outside** the body to treat infections. They work by killing the infectious organism or stopping it from **breathing / growing**. Antibiotics that are used to treat bacterial infections are called **antibacterials / probacterials**. Antifungals are used to treat **fungal / viral** infections. Antibiotics **can / cannot** be used to treat viral infections.

Q2 **Antiseptics** are found in many household products.

a) Suggest a household product that is likely to contain antiseptics.

....

b) What is an antiseptic?

....

c) How are antiseptics used?

....

....

Q3 Some **plants** produce chemicals.

a) Why might plants produce chemicals that have antibacterial effects?

....

b) Give an example of a plant chemical which has antibacterial effects that humans use.

....

Antiseptics and Antibiotics

Q1 The graph shows the number of bacteria in Gary's blood during a two-week course of **antibiotics**.

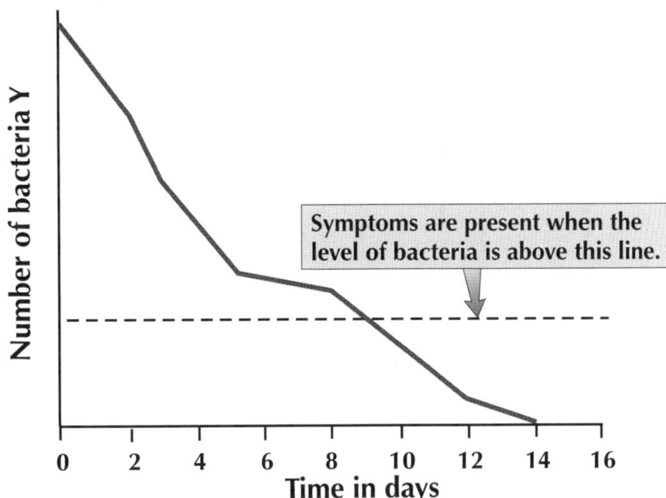

a) Define the term "antibiotic".

....

b) How long after starting the course of antibiotics will Gary's symptoms disappear? ....

c) Why is it important for Gary to **finish** his full course of antibiotics?

....

d) Give an **example** of a strain of bacteria that is resistant to antibiotics.

....

Q2 Jenny went to the doctor because she had **flu**. The doctor advised her to stay in bed for a while but didn't give her any antibiotics.

a) Why wouldn't the doctor give her any antibiotics for her condition?

....

b) Explain how bacteria can develop **resistance** to an antibiotic.

....

....

....

....

Top Tips: Antibiotics are just great but they should be used with care as nobody wants a nasty superbug hanging around, bugging everyone. You need to know how these can develop. So learn it.

Antiseptics and Antibiotics

Q3 In 1960, a **new antibiotic** was discovered which was very effective against **disease X**. Doctors have been prescribing this drug ever since. The graph below shows the number of deaths from disease X over a number of years.

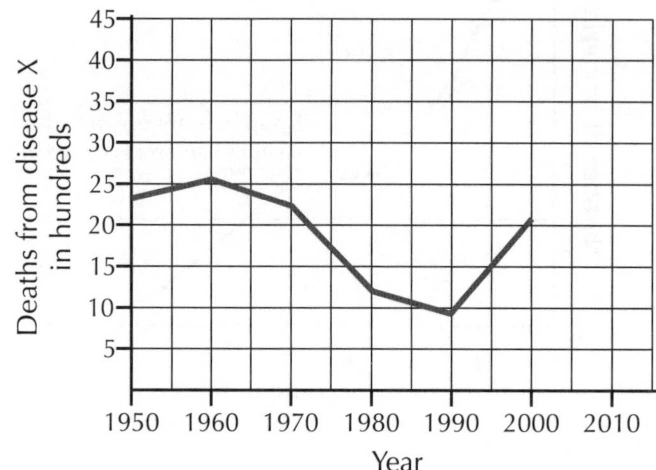

a) Assuming nothing changes, use the graph to **predict** the number of deaths from disease X in **2010**.

....

b) Suggest a reason for the **fall** in deaths from the disease between 1960 and 1990.

....

c) Suggest a reason for the **sudden rise** in deaths from the disease between 1990 and 2000.

....

....

Q4 Gavin and Van carried out an experiment at school to investigate the effectiveness of five different **antiseptics** (1–5). They spread some bacteria onto a sterile agar plate. They then placed discs of filter paper, impregnated with the five different antiseptics, onto the bacterial culture.

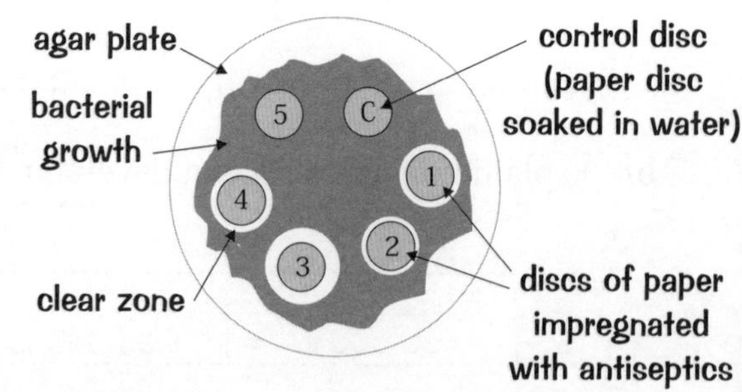

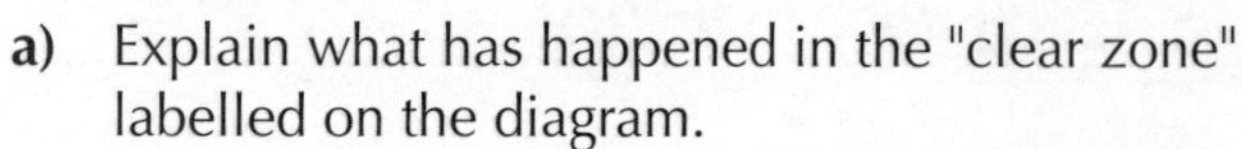

a) Explain what has happened in the "clear zone" labelled on the diagram.

....

b) Which of the antiseptics (1–5) was the most effective against these bacteria? ....

Energy and Biomass

Q1 Complete the sentences below by **circling** the most appropriate word each time.

a) **Plants** / **Animals** can make their own food by a process called **photosynthesis** / **respiration**.

b) To obtain energy animals must **decay** / **eat** plant material or other animals.

c) Animals release energy from food through the process of **photosynthesis** / **respiration**.

d) Some of the energy obtained by animals from their food is **gained** / **lost** before it reaches organisms at later steps of the food chain. This is mainly because it has been used for **growth** / **movement**.

Q2 Read the sentences below about **food chains, energy transfer** and **pyramids of biomass**. Then tick the boxes to show which sentences are true and which are false.

		True	False
a)	Plants convert all the light energy that falls on them into glucose.	☐	☐
b)	Energy is used in respiration at each stage in a food chain.	☐	☐
c)	Only energy is passed between the steps of food chains.	☐	☐
d)	Animals that have to maintain a constant body temperature lose more energy as heat than animals that don't.	☐	☐
e)	Pyramids of biomass always start with a producer.	☐	☐
f)	Pyramids of biomass can only have three steps.	☐	☐

Q3 A **food chain** is shown below.

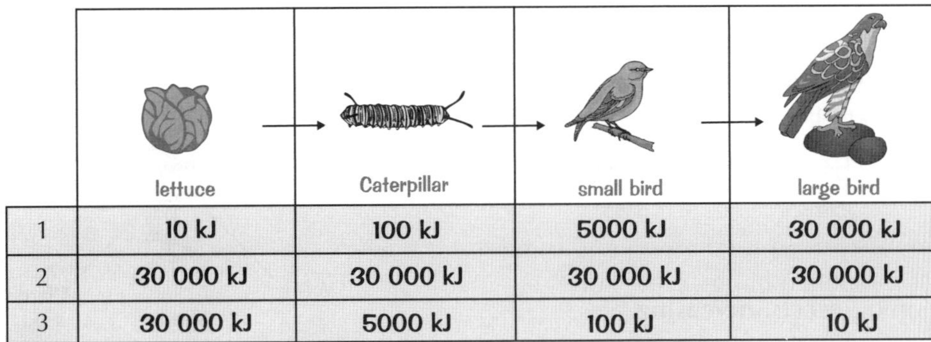

	lettuce	Caterpillar	small bird	large bird
1	10 kJ	100 kJ	5000 kJ	30 000 kJ
2	30 000 kJ	30 000 kJ	30 000 kJ	30 000 kJ
3	30 000 kJ	5000 kJ	100 kJ	10 kJ

a) Which row, 1, 2 or 3, shows the amount of energy available at each trophic level? ....

b) Explain your reasoning for part **a)**.

....

Energy and Biomass

Q4 A single **robin** has a mass of 15 g and eats caterpillars. Each robin eats 25 **caterpillars** that each have a mass of 2 g. The caterpillars feed on 10 **stinging nettles** that together have a mass of 500 g. Study the pyramid diagrams shown and then answer the questions that follow.

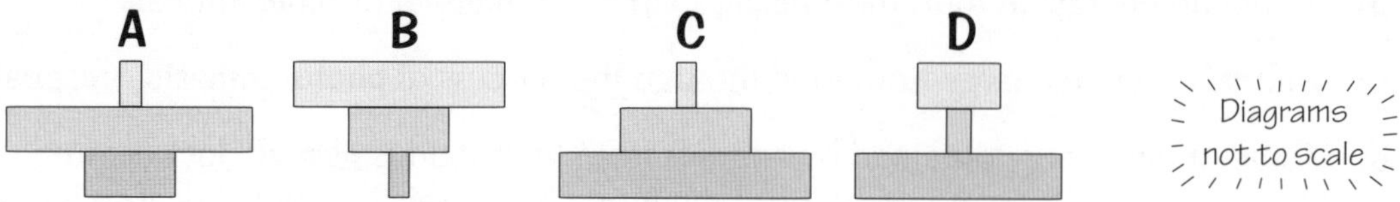

a) Which diagram is most likely to represent a pyramid of biomass for these organisms? ....

b) Explain how you decided on your answer to part **a)** above.

....

....

c) The stinging nettles are the first trophic level. Where does their energy initially come from?

....

d) Explain why food chains rarely have more than five trophic levels.

....

....

Q5 The **food web** below shows how species in a woodland are **interdependent**.

a) What is meant by the term "interdependent"?

....

....

b) Last year a chemical was spilt in the woods, and turned out to be poisonous to voles. The population of **voles** significantly **decreased**. Suggest an explanation for each of the following consequences:

i) The population of barn owls **decreasing**.

....

ii) The population of insects **increasing**.

....

iii) The population of insects **decreasing**.

....

Barn owl
Vole
Insects
Bird
Grass and seeds

Parasitism and Mutualism

Q1 **Parasitism** and **mutualism** are both ways that one species can depend on another species.

a) In a **parasitic relationship** one organism benefits.
What is the name given to the **other** organism in the relationship?

....

b) Put a tick in the box next to the statement that correctly describes **mutualism**.

☐ one organism benefits and the other is neither helped nor harmed

☐ one organism benefits and the other is harmed

☐ both organisms benefit from the relationship

Q2 Draw a line to match each **parasite** with its effect on other organisms.

Mistletoe	Live in the fur and bedding of animals, and feed by sucking their blood.
Tapeworms	Live on human scalps and suck their blood, making them itch.
Fleas	Attach to an animal's intestinal wall and absorb lots of nutrients.
Head lice	Grows on trees and shrubs, absorbing water and nutrients from them.

Q3 The pairs of organisms below have a **mutualistic relationship**.
For each organism state what, if anything, it **gains** from the relationship.

a) oxpeckers ....

buffalo ....

b) nitrogen-fixing bacteria ....

legumes ....

c) chemosynthetic bacteria ....

deep-sea vent tubeworms ....

d) cleaner wrasse (cleaner fish) ....

grouper (larger host fish) ....

Top Tips: An outbreak of head lice is great news for the lice, but bad news for everyone else. This kind of relationship is the same for all parasites — one species thrives while another is harmed.

Human Activity and the Environment

Q1 The size of **Earth's population** has an impact on our environment.

a) How would you expect an **increase** in population size to affect the following things?

i) The amount of **raw materials** (including non-renewable energy resources)

....

ii) **Waste disposal**

....

b) Many human activities cause pollution.
Name a **man-made source** of each of the following pollutants:

i) phosphate ....

ii) nitrate ....

iii) sulfur dioxide ....

Q2 The size of the **Earth's population** has changed dramatically in the last 1000 years.

a) Use the table below to plot a graph on the grid, showing how the world's human population has changed over the last 1000 years.

Population size / billions	Year
0.3	1000
0.4	1200
0.4	1400
0.6	1600
1.0	1800
1.7	1900
6.1	2000

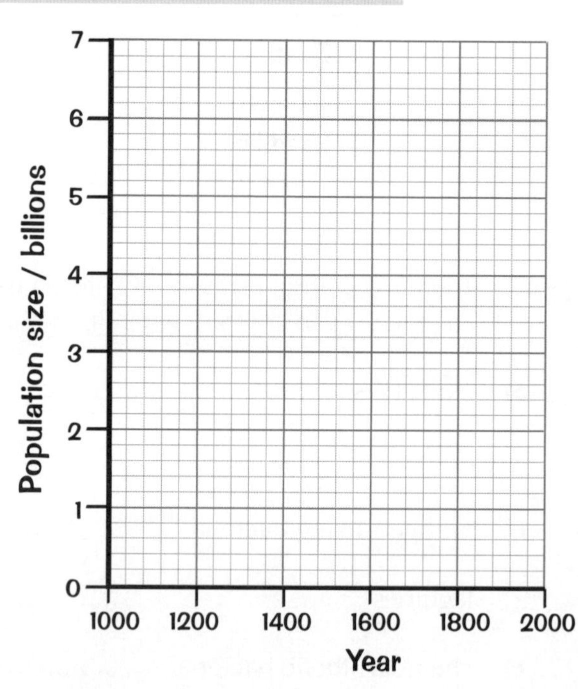

b) Circle the correct word to complete each sentence.

i) The size of the Earth's population now is **bigger** / **smaller** than it was 1000 years ago.

ii) The growth of the population now is **slower** / **faster** than it was 1000 years ago.

iii) The impact on the environment now is **less** / **greater** than it was 1000 years ago.

c) Suggest **two** reasons for the sudden increase in the population.

....

....

Human Activity and the Environment

Q3 Rivers and lakes can be **polluted** by **fertilisers** that come from nearby farmland. This often results in the death of many fish.

a) Why are fertilisers essential to modern farming?

....

b) How does the fertiliser get into the rivers and lakes?

....

c) How does pollution by fertilisers cause fish to die?

....

....

....

d) What is the name given to this type of pollution by fertilisers?

....

Q4 A student decided to test the effect of **nitrate fertiliser** on plant growth. She placed **four seeds** into four different Petri dishes. Each dish contained cotton wool soaked in **different concentrations** of nitrate. The results are shown below.

A: no nitrate

C: high nitrate concentration

B: low nitrate concentration

D: very high nitrate concentration

a) Which Petri dish was the control? ....

b) Briefly describe the effects of nitrate fertiliser on plant growth in this experiment.

....

....

....

Recycling

Q1 Tick the boxes to show which of the following are good reasons for **recycling metals**.

- [ ] The recycling process gives many metals useful new properties.
- [ ] It uses less energy and therefore less fossil fuel.
- [ ] The metal produced is purer and so of a higher quality.
- [ ] Less carbon dioxide is produced as a result.

Q2 There are important **benefits** of recycling, but it is still **not** a perfect solution.

a) Explain how recycling materials helps to conserve the world's energy resources.

....

....

b) State three ways in which the recycling process uses energy.

1. ....

2. ....

3. ....

Q3 Explain each of the following statements about **recycling**.

a) Recycling **plastic** can help tackle the problem of waste disposal.

....

....

....

b) Recycling **paper** can help to reduce global warming.

Think about the carbon cycle.

....

....

....

Top Tips: The UK isn't great at recycling — we're getting better, but still languishing far behind other European countries. Collection schemes are making things easier, so no more excuses.

Indicator Species

Q1 **Stonefly larvae** and **sludge worms** are often studied to see how much **sewage** is in water. Juanita took samples of water from where two different drains empty into a river. She recorded the number of each species in the water samples and her results are shown below.

Site	No. of stonefly larvae	No. of sludge worms
After drain A	22	0
After drain B	0	30

a) Which drain(s) seem to be polluting the river with sewage?
Circle the correct answer: **Neither Drain / Drain A / Drain B / Drains A and B**

b) Suggest **two** other indicator species that Juanita could have studied instead.

1. .... 2. ....

Q2 The number of species of **lichen** living in an area can be used as an **indicator** of how **clean** the air is there. Scientists did a survey of the number of lichens found on gravestones at different distances from a city centre. The results are shown below:

Distance from city centre (km)	No. of species found on ten gravestones
0	12
2	13
6	22
16	29
20	30
24	35

No. of species of lichen

Distance from city centre (km)

a) Draw a graph of this data on the grid provided.

b) What **general trend** is shown by the data?

....

....

c) Give a possible **reason** for this trend.

....

....

d) Name **another species** that can be used to indicate clean air.

....

The Carbon Cycle

Q1 Complete the diagram below as instructed to show a **part** of the **carbon cycle**.

CO_2 in the air

plant

animal

a) Add an arrow or arrows labelled **P** to represent **photosynthesis**.

b) Add an arrow or arrows labelled **R** to represent **respiration**.

c) Add an arrow or arrows labelled **F** to represent **feeding**.

Q2 Answer the following questions to show how the **stages** in the **carbon cycle** are ordered.

a) Number the sentences below to show how carbon moves between the air and living things. The first one has been done for you.

.... Animals eat the plants' carbon compounds.

.....1...... Carbon dioxide in the air.

.... Plants and animals die.

.... Plants take in carbon dioxide for photosynthesis and make carbon compounds.

b) Add a point 5 to complete the cycle and show how carbon is returned to the air.

Point 5: ....

Q3 Answer the following questions about the **carbon cycle**.

a) What is the most common form of carbon found in the atmosphere?

....

b) What products do plants convert this carbon into?

....

c) How is the carbon in plants passed on through the food chain?

....

d) Give **three** things that can happen to dead plants and animals.

1. ....

2. ....

3. ....

The Carbon Cycle

Q4 The diagram below shows one version of the **carbon cycle**.

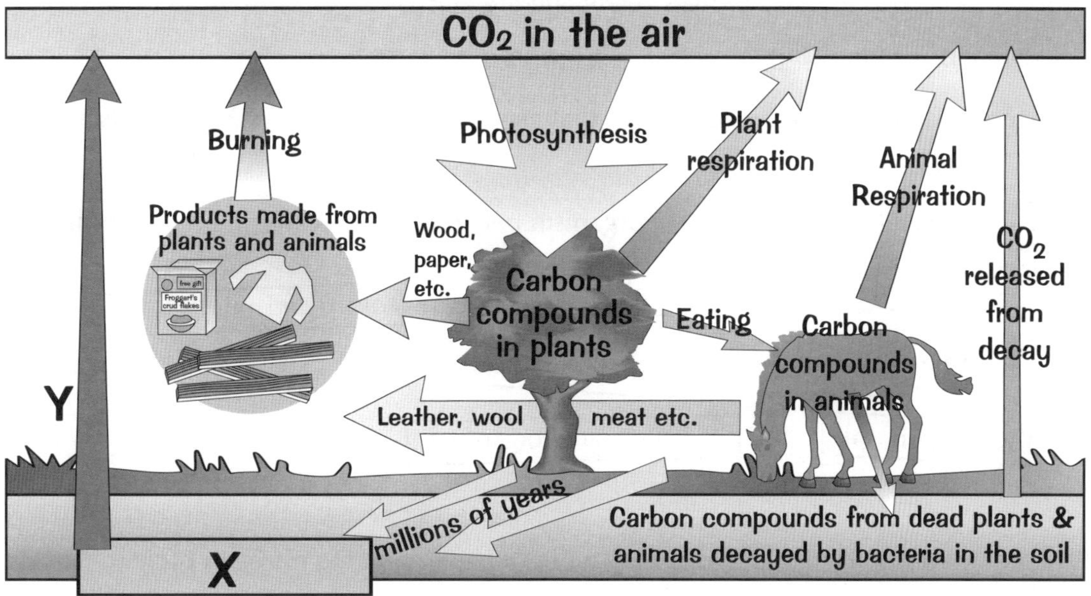

a) Name substance **X** shown on the diagram above. ....

b) Explain why substance **X** contains carbon.

....

....

c) Name the process labelled **Y** on the diagram above. ....

Q5 Nutrients are constantly **recycled**.

a) Name **three** elements (other than carbon) that are recycled in the environment.

....

b) Explain why **microorganisms** are important in recycling nutrients.

Don't just describe what the microorganisms do — explain why it's important.

....

....

....

Top Tips: Lots of substances are **recycled**, not just carbon. They enter organisms when they feed (or photosynthesise) and leave when they die, breathe or poo. That's the great circle of life for you.

The Nitrogen Cycle

Q1 Circle the correct word or phrase to complete the following sentences.

a) Nitrogen is needed to make **protein** / **carbohydrate** / **fat**.

b) The percentage of the air that is nitrogen is **100%** / **21%** / **78%**.

c) Nitrogen is **a reactive** / **an unreactive** gas that **can** / **can't** be used directly by plants and animals.

Q2 Draw lines to match up each type of **organism** below with the way that it obtains **nitrogen**.

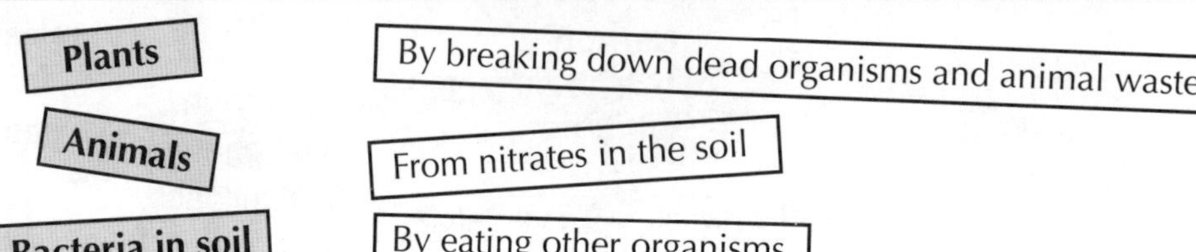

Q3 Explain the role of each of the following types of **bacteria** in the **nitrogen cycle**.

a) Decomposer bacteria ....

b) Nitrifying bacteria ....

c) Nitrogen-fixing bacteria ....

Q4 Below is a diagram of the **nitrogen cycle**. Explain what is shown by the arrows labelled:

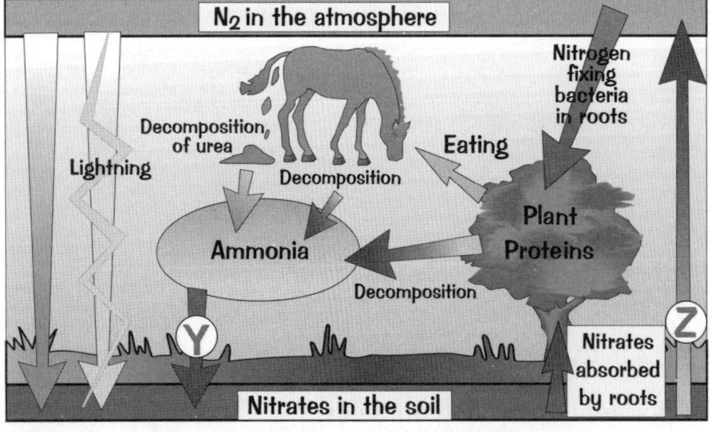

a) Y ....

....

....

b) Z ....

....

....

c) What role does lightning play in the nitrogen cycle?

....

Q5 A farmer was told that if he planted **legume plants** his soil would be more **fertile**. Explain how the legume plants would increase the fertility of the soil.

....

....

Mixed Questions — B1 Topic 3

Q1 **Malaria** is a disease that is common in tropical areas.

a) Fill in the blanks in the paragraph using some of the words from the list below.

mosquitoes guest agent old biting killed insecticide

kissing vector protozoan dirty water lymph chump

Malaria is a disease caused by a .... The infection is transmitted from person to person by ...., which spread the disease by .... people. An organism which transfers a disease without actually getting it is called a ....

b) Mosquito coils release smoke that deters mosquitoes.
However, they also contain carcinogens. What is a carcinogen?

....

c) Quinine is a drug that protects against malaria. In the past it was taken as a tonic mixed with gin, which is an alcoholic drink.

i) What type of drug is alcohol?

....

ii) How does this type of drug affect the brain?

....

....

Q2 **Infectious** diseases are diseases which are **transmitted** from one person to another.

a) What is a pathogen?

....

b) Name **four** types of pathogen.

....

c) All pathogens are parasites. What does this mean?

....

d) How does the respiratory system use physical barriers to stop pathogens from entering the body?

....

....

Mixed Questions — B1 Topic 3

Q3 Human activity causes various types of **air pollution**. Three common air pollutants are:

Carbon dioxide **Carbon monoxide** **Sulfur dioxide**

Each statement below refers to one or more of these pollutants.
Indicate which one(s) in the space provided.

a) May be released when fossil fuels are burnt. ....

b) A poisonous gas that prevents red blood cells carrying oxygen. ....

c) Kills blackspot fungi on rose leaves. ....

d) Removed from the air by photosynthesis. ....

Q4 **Legumes** are plants that have nodules on their roots containing **nitrogen-fixing bacteria**.

a) Plants absorb nitrogen compounds from the soil. What is the name of these nitrogen compounds?

....

b) Explain why plants can't get their nitrogen directly from the air.

....

....

c) The legumes and the nitrogen-fixing bacteria have a mutualistic relationship.
Explain fully what this means.

....

....

Q5 **Air pollution** can be measured using both **living** and **non-living indicators**.

a) Explain what each of these methods involve.

....

....

....

b) A sample of **lichens** is taken from trees in two different towns. The sample from **town A** contains 19 organisms of 2 different lichen species. The sample from **town B** contain 36 organisms of 8 different lichen species. Which town do you think is the more polluted? Explain your answer.

....

....

Mixed Questions — B1 Topic 3

Q6 The diagram below shows a **food chain** observed on the savannahs of Tanzania. It also shows the amount of **energy** available in each trophic level.

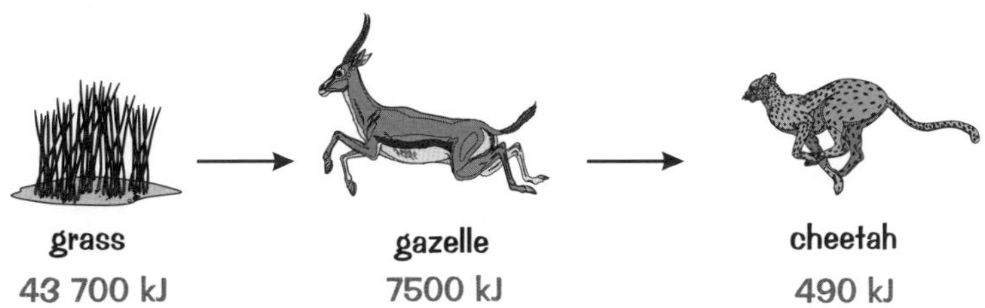

a) Where does the grass get its energy from?

....

b) Suggest **two** ways in which energy might be lost by the gazelle.

....

....

c) **Carbon** also moves through the food chain. It is continuously being **recycled** from one form to another as the diagram below shows.

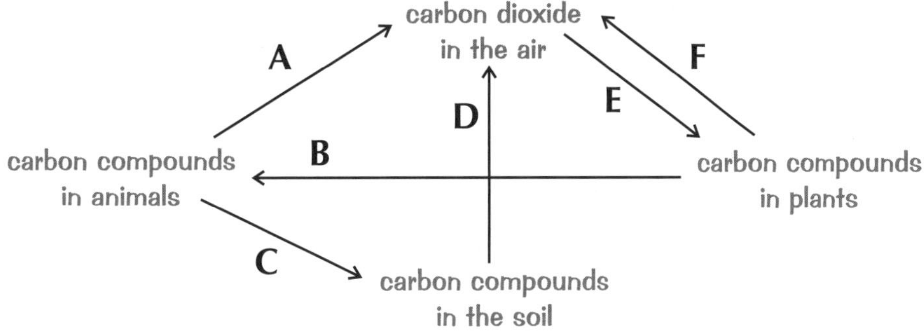

Name the processes labelled **A**, **B**, **C**, **D**, **E** and **F** in the diagram.

A .... B ....

C .... D ....

E .... F ....

d) Also growing on the savannah are Acacia trees which belong to the legume family. They contain bacteria in nodules in their roots, and transfer sugar to the bacteria. The bacteria use this sugar in their respiration. Using this information, add the following arrows and labels to the correct places in the carbon cycle diagram above:

carbon compounds in bacteria   transfer of sugar →   respiration →

Mixed Questions — B1 Topic 3

Q7 **Athlete's foot** is caused by a microorganism that infects the skin. The disease is treated by applying **antifungal compounds**.

a) State the type of microorganism that causes athlete's foot.

....

b) Explain how the microorganism is transmitted.

....

....

c) The diagram below shows the results of an experiment to test extracts from different plants for their potential **antifungal properties**. Discs containing different plant extracts dissolved in ethanol were put onto a Petri dish that had been evenly spread with microbes. The microbes were allowed to grow.

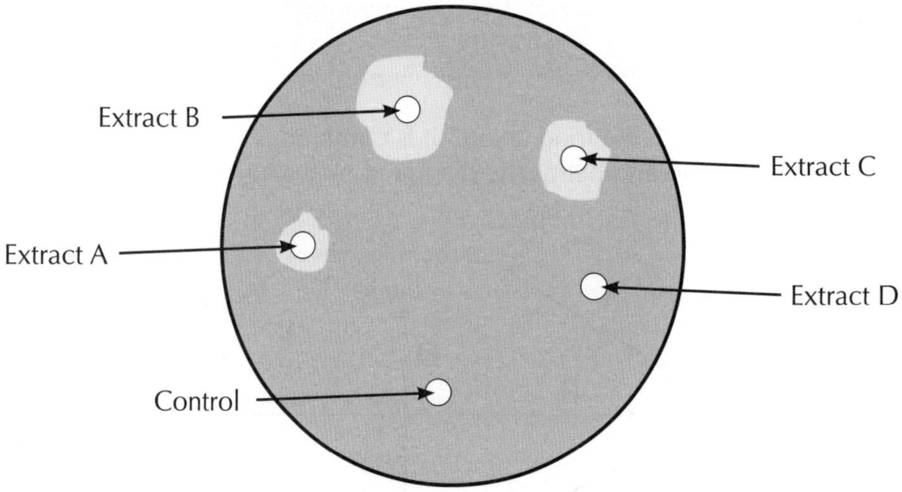

i) What should the control disc be soaked in?

....

ii) Which extract was the **most** effective?

....

iii) Which extract was the **least** effective?

....

iv) Give **three** variables that should be controlled in this experiment.

1. ....

2. ....

3. ....

Cells and Microscopy

Q1 Plant and animal cells have **similarities** and **differences**.
Complete each statement below by circling the correct words.

a) **Plant** / **Animal** cells, but not **plant** / **animal** cells, contain chloroplasts.

b) Plant cells have **vacuoles** / **cytoplasm** containing cell sap.

c) **Both plant and animal cells** / **Only plant cells** / **Only animal cells** have cell membranes.

d) The **cytoplasm** / **nucleus** is the gel-like part of the cell, where most of the chemical reactions happen.

Q2 Draw lines to match up each **part** of a bacterium to its correct **description**.

Flagellum	DNA that controls the cell's activities, found in the cytoplasm
Plasmid	small loop of DNA that can be passed between bacteria
Chromosomal DNA	helps the cell to move

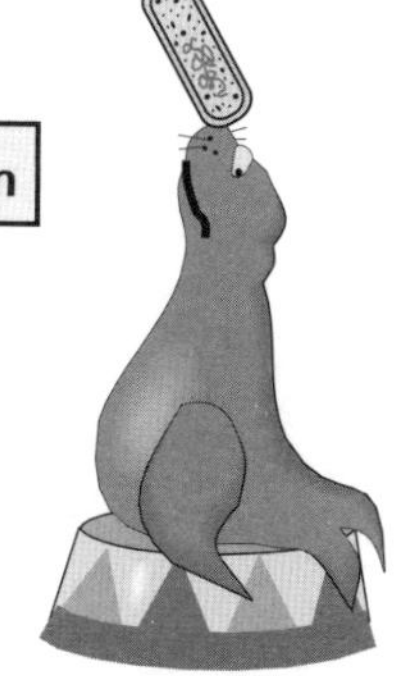

Q3 This question is about the **parts** of a cell.

a) State what each of the following cell structures contains or is made of.

i) The **nucleus** contains ....

ii) **Chloroplasts** contain ....

iii) The **cell wall** is made of ....

b) Describe the functions of these parts of the cell.

i) The **nucleus** ....

ii) **Chloroplasts** ....

iii) The **cell wall** ....

iv) The **cell membrane** ....

v) **Mitochondria** ....

Q4 The diagram shows a typical **bacterium**.

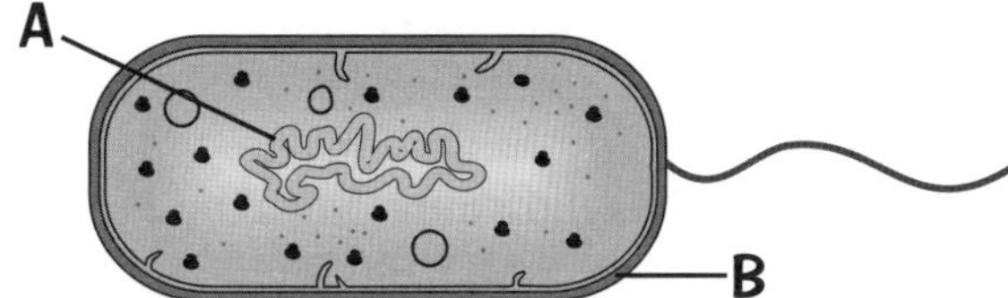

a) Name parts A and B on the diagram.

A ....

B ....

b) Name **one** feature of a typical plant cell that is not seen in bacterial cells.

....

Cells and Microscopy

Q5 **Microscopes** let us see things that we can't see with the naked eye.

a) A picture of a light microscope is shown below.

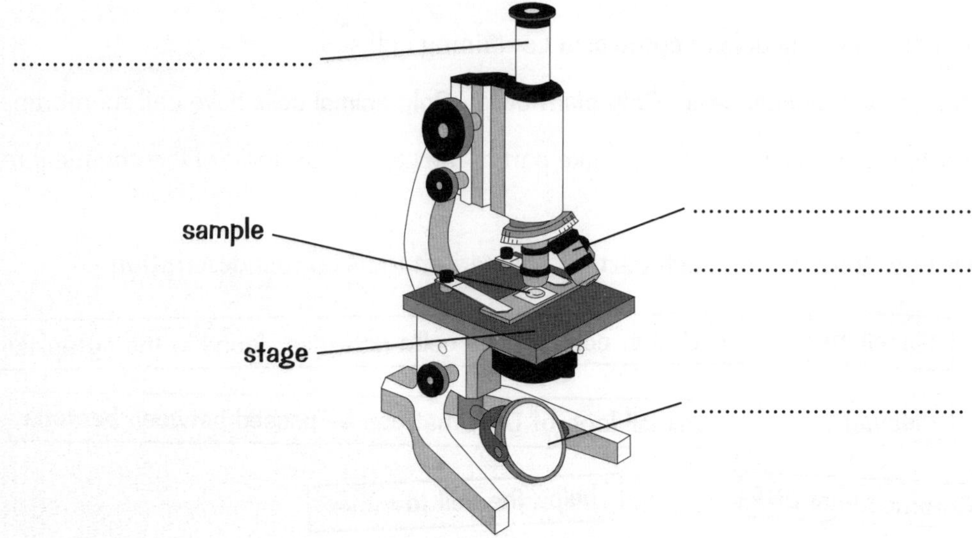

i) Complete the missing labels on the picture of the microscope.

ii) Circle the parts of the microscope you would use to focus your image.

b) Name **two** plant cell structures that you'd be able to see using a light microscope.

1. ....

2. ....

c) Name **one** type of microscope, other than a light microscope.

....

Q6 Professor Smart has invented a shrinking ray. He tests it on his cat, Fluffy, by shrinking him down to **0.06 mm long**.

a) The Professor looks at Fluffy using a **light microscope**. The image that he sees is **9 mm long**. Calculate the magnification of Professor Smart's image.

....

....

b) Fluffy's tail is **0.02 mm** long. The Professor now looks at him using **× 300** magnification. Calculate how long Fluffy's tail will be on the magnified image.

....

....

DNA

Q1 The following questions are about **DNA**.

a) What name is given to the shape of a DNA molecule? ....

b) How many different **bases** are there in DNA? ....

c) Which bases pair up together?

....

d) What type of bonds hold the base pairs together? ....

Q2 You can extract **DNA** from **onion cells** in a simple experiment in the lab.

a) The steps of this experiment are shown below.
Put them in the correct order by numbering the boxes. The first one has been done for you.

- [ ] Cool the mixture down again and filter it.
- [ ] Put the beaker into a water bath at 60 °C for 15 minutes.
- [ ] Add ice-cold alcohol to the filtered mixture. When the DNA has come out of solution, fish it out using a glass rod.
- [1] Chop the onion. Put it in a beaker with a solution of detergent and salt.
- [ ] Once the mixture is ice-cold, put it into a blender for a few seconds.
- [ ] Put the beaker in ice to cool the mixture down.

b) Explain why the mixture is heated to 60 °C for 15 minutes.

....

....

Q3 Complete the passage about the **discovery of DNA** using some of the words below.

light equal to Rosalind Franklin X-rays Francis Crick less than half

.... and Maurice Wilkins worked out that DNA has a helical structure by directing beams of .... onto crystallised DNA and looking at the patterns they made as they bounced off. James Watson and .... used these ideas, plus the fact that the amount of adenine + guanine is .... the amount of thymine + cytosine, to make a model of the DNA molecule.

Top Tips: Your DNA controls what proteins your cells make — and they control everything the cells do. That's why the discovery of the structure of DNA was such a massive breakthrough in biology.

Protein Synthesis

Q1 Tick the boxes to show whether the following statements are **true** or **false**.

		True	False
a)	Genes are sections of DNA that code for specific proteins.	☐	☐
b)	Each amino acid is coded for by a set of four base pairs.	☐	☐
c)	The order of bases in a gene determines the order of amino acids.	☐	☐
d)	mRNA contains two strands, like DNA.	☐	☐
e)	Translation takes place in the nucleus.	☐	☐
f)	Amino acids join together to make polypeptides.	☐	☐
g)	Each protein is made with a unique number and sequence of amino acids — this is what determines its shape and function.	☐	☐

Q2 On the section of **DNA** shown:

A G G C T A G C C A A T C G C C G A A G C T C A

T C C G A T C G G T T A G C G

a) Finish the lower sequence of bases.

b) Calculate how many amino acids are coded for by this section of DNA.

....

Q3 Genes can have **mutations** in them.

a) What are mutations?

....

b) Are mutations always harmful? Explain your answer.

....

Q4 **mRNA** is a messenger molecule used by the cell as a template for making **proteins**.

a) **i)** How is a molecule of mRNA formed from a molecule of DNA?

....

....

ii) Is this step called transcription or translation? ....

b) How do mRNA and ribosomes work together to build proteins?

....

....

....

....

Enzymes

Q1 a) Write a definition of the word 'enzyme'.

....

b) In the space below, draw a sketch to show how an enzyme's **shape** allows it to break substances down.

c) For an enzyme to work, the substrate must **fit exactly** into its active site. Give the name for this type of mechanism.

....

Q2 Draw lines to match the words below about **enzyme action** with their meanings.

active site	the chemical substance that an enzyme works on
specificity	the idea that enzymes only work with one substrate
substrate	the part of an enzyme which the substrate attaches to

Q3 **Enzymes** are involved in all sorts of reactions in the body, both **outside** and **inside cells.**

a) Name **one** type of reaction catalysed by enzymes that takes place **outside** cells.

....

b) Name **two** types of reaction catalysed by enzymes that take place **inside** cells.

....

Q4 Briefly describe how you could use **iodine solution** to measure the rate of an enzyme-controlled reaction.

....

....

....

More On Enzymes

Q1 Tick the correct boxes to show whether the sentences are **true** or **false**.

		True	False
a)	You can investigate the effect of temperature on enzymes by using different water baths.	☐	☐
b)	The rate of most chemical reactions can be increased by lowering the temperature.	☐	☐
c)	Most cells are damaged at very high temperatures.	☐	☐
d)	Each enzyme has its own optimum temperature and pH, where it is most active.	☐	☐
e)	All enzymes work best at neutral pH.	☐	☐

Q2 This graph shows the results from an investigation into the effect of **temperature** on the rate of an **enzyme** catalysed reaction.

Rate of Reaction
0
45
Temperature (°C)

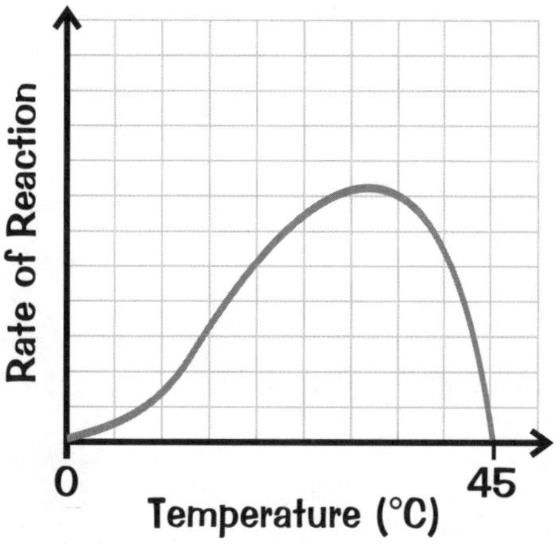

a) What is the **optimum** temperature for this enzyme?

....

b) Describe what happens to the structure of an enzyme at temperatures **above** its optimum.

....

....

....

Q3 The graph on the right shows how the **rate** of an enzyme-catalysed reaction is affected by **substrate concentration**.

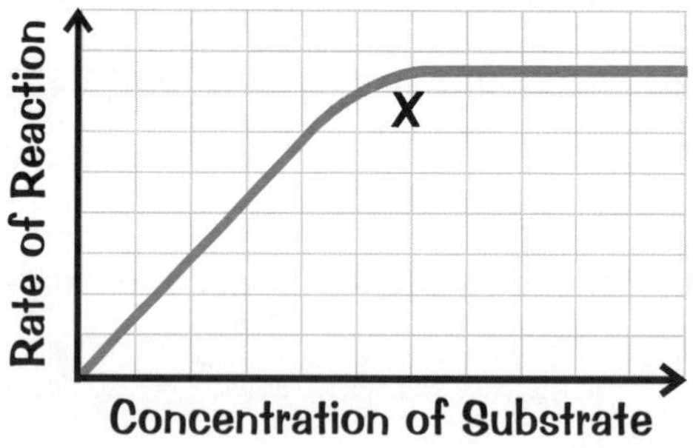

Rate of Reaction
X
Concentration of Substrate

a) Explain why the graph climbs steeply at first.

....

....

....

b) Explain why the graph levels off after point X.

....

....

....

More On Enzymes

Q4 Stuart has a sample of an enzyme and he is trying to find out what its **optimum pH** is. Stuart tests the enzyme by **timing** how long it takes to break down a substance at different pH levels. The results of Stuart's experiment are shown below.

pH	Time taken for reaction (seconds)
2	101
4	83
6	17
8	76
10	99
12	102

a) Draw a line graph of the results on the grid below.

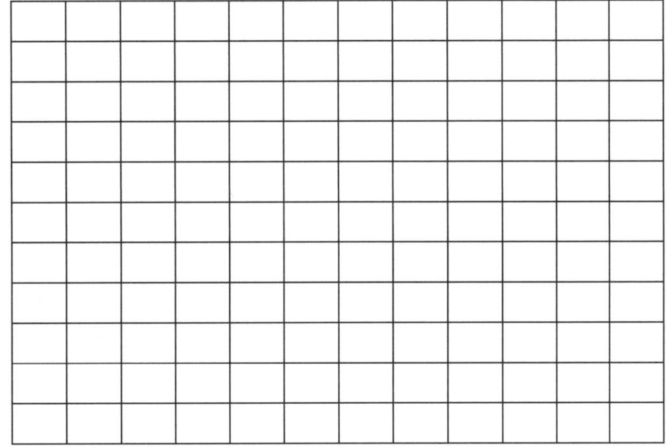

b) Roughly what is the **optimum** pH for the enzyme?

....

c) Explain why the reaction is very slow at certain pH levels.

....

d) Would you expect to find this enzyme in the stomach? Explain your answer.

....

e) Describe two things that Stuart would need to do to make sure his experiment is a fair test.

1. ....

2. ....

Top Tips: Enzymes crop up a lot in Biology so it's worth spending plenty of time making sure you know all the basics. If you're finding things a bit dull, you could always take a little break and eat some tofu to make sure you have enough protein to make lots of delightful enzymes.

The Human Genome Project

Q1 Tick the boxes to show whether these statements about the **human genome** are **true** or **false**.

		True	False
a)	The aim of the Human Genome Project was to find all of the 25 000 or so human genes.	☐	☐
b)	Thousands of scientists worldwide collaborated on the Human Genome Project.	☐	☐
c)	Scientists now know the function of every one of the human genes.	☐	☐

Q2 The Human Genome Project could lead to big improvements in **medical treatment**.

a) Explain how information about a person's genes could be used to **prevent** diseases.

....

....

b) Explain how information about a person's genes could be used to **treat** diseases.

....

....

Q3 Soon it may be possible to test a person's DNA to find out if they are likely to suffer from heart disease. Marco's genotype makes it likely that he will suffer from **heart disease** at an early age. Explain how it could have a **negative effect** on Marco if this fact was made available to:

a) an **employer** who was about to offer him a job.

....

b) an **insurance company** who were about to give him life insurance.

....

c) Marco himself.

....

Q4 Police investigators can analyse DNA samples taken from the scene of a **crime** and compare this to the DNA of a **suspect**. In the future, it may be possible to look at the DNA samples from the crime scene and work out from them what the suspect **looks like**.

a) Underline any of the following characteristics that could be deduced from a person's DNA.

i) whether they have blue or brown eyes. **ii)** whether they have a scar on their cheek.

iii) whether they are male or female. **iv)** whether they are fat or thin.

b) Explain **why** some characteristics could be worked out from the DNA, but others could not.

....

....

Genetic Engineering

Q1 Fill in the gaps in the passage below to explain **how** genetic engineering is carried out.

The useful .... is 'cut' out from one organism's chromosome using .... Enzymes are then used to cut another organism's chromosome and the useful .... is inserted. This technique produces .... organisms.

Q2 Genetic engineering is used to produce **human insulin**.

a) What type of organism is genetically modified to make human insulin?

....

b) Explain why producing insulin in this way can benefit humans.

....

....

Q3 **Golden Rice** was developed in order to increase the amount of **vitamin A** that could be obtained from a rice crop. It is estimated that a person would only have to eat **144 g** of Golden Rice per day in order to receive the recommended daily allowance of vitamin A, compared with **2.3 kg** of natural basmati rice.

a) The new genes introduced into the Golden Rice plant make it produce a chemical that the humans body turns into vitamin A. Give the name of this chemical.

....

b) Calculate how much **more** natural basmati rice you need to eat than Golden Rice to get your recommended daily allowance of vitamin A.

....

c) It has been suggested that Golden Rice would be very useful as a crop in developing countries. Explain why it might be useful in such countries.

....

....

Top Tips: Before some clever-clogs worked out how to genetically modify organisms to make it, insulin for diabetics had to be extracted from animals and purified. Not easy, and not a nice thought for the diabetics either. So being able to make pure insulin in the lab was a real breakthrough.

Genetic Engineering

Q4 A crop plant had been genetically modified to make it **resistant to herbicides**. Some people were **concerned** that, as a result, wild grasses growing nearby might also become resistant to herbicides. Scientists decided to check whether this had happened.

The scientists sprayed herbicide onto 100 plants in an area next to the GM crop, and onto 100 plants from a second area far away from the GM crop.

Their results are shown in the table below.

Number of grass plants dying after spraying	
In area next to GM crop	In area far away from GM crop
83	85

a) Explain the reason for testing a group of plants that had not been growing near the GM crop.

....

....

b) How could the scientists have made the results of this experiment **more reliable**?

....

c) The scientists decided that there was no significant difference between the two groups of plants. Explain whether you agree or disagree with this conclusion.

....

....

....

d) If the scientists are right in their conclusion, does this prove that the concerns about genes for resistance spreading are unfounded? Explain your answer.

....

....

....

e) If wild grasses become resistant to herbicides, what **problems** might this cause?

....

....

Mitosis

Q1 Tick the boxes to show whether the following statements are **true** or **false**.

		True	False
a)	Human body cells are diploid.	☐	☐
b)	There are 20 pairs of chromosomes in a human cheek cell.	☐	☐
c)	Chromosomes are found in the cytoplasm of a cell.	☐	☐
d)	Before a cell divides by mitosis, it duplicates its DNA.	☐	☐
e)	Mitosis is where a cell splits to create two genetically identical copies.	☐	☐
f)	Each new cell produced in mitosis gets one chromosome from each pair.	☐	☐
g)	Organisms use mitosis in order to grow.	☐	☐
h)	Organisms do not use mitosis to replace damaged cells.	☐	☐

Q2 The following diagram shows the different stages of **mitosis**.
Write a short description to explain each stage.

a) ....

b) ....

c) ....
....

d) ....
....

e) ....

Q3 Complete the following passage using the words below.

runners **strawberry** **variation** **asexual** **reproduce** **genes**

Some organisms use mitosis to .... For example, ... plants produce .... this way, which become new plants. This is known as .... reproduction. The offspring have exactly the same .... as the parent, which means there's no genetic ....

Meiosis

Q1 Circle the correct word from each pair to complete the sentences below.

a) Gametes are sex cells. During **asexual** / **sexual** reproduction two gametes combine to form a new cell that will grow into a new organism.

b) Gametes are **diploid** / **haploid**. This means they have **one copy** / **two copies** of each chromosome. This is so that when two gametes combine the resulting cell has the right number of chromosomes.

c) Human body cells have **23** / **46** chromosomes and human gametes have **23** / **46** chromosomes. When the gametes combine you get **23** / **46** chromosomes again.

Q2 Tick the boxes to show whether the following statements are **true** or **false**.

		True	False
a)	Meiosis halves the number of chromosomes.	☐	☐
b)	Meiosis forms gametes that are genetically identical.	☐	☐
c)	In humans, meiosis only happens in the reproductive organs.	☐	☐
d)	At fertilisation, two haploid gametes join to form a diploid zygote.	☐	☐

Q3 Draw lines to match each description of the stage of **meiosis** to the right diagram below.

a) 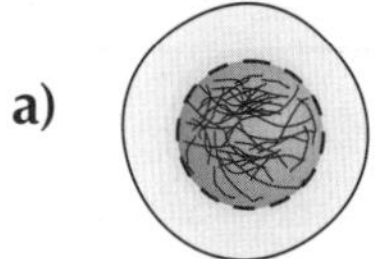

b)

c) 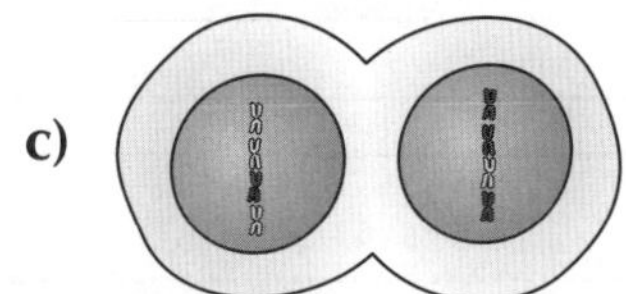

d) 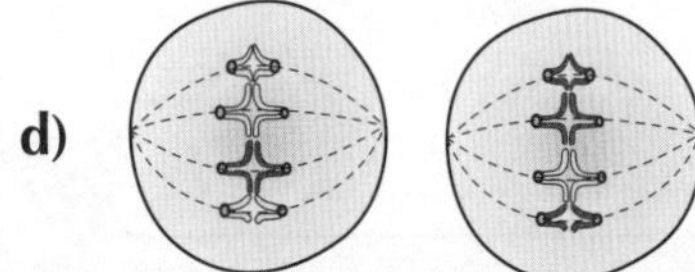

e) 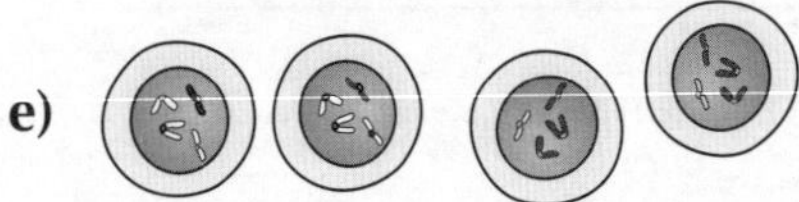

The pairs are pulled apart, mixing up the mother and father's chromosomes into the new cells. This creates genetic variation.

Before the cell starts to divide it duplicates its DNA to produce an exact copy.

There are now 4 gametes, each containing half the original number of chromosomes.

For the first meiotic division the chromosomes line up in their pairs across the centre of the cell.

The chromosomes line up across the centre of the nucleus ready for the second division, and the two arms of each chromosome are pulled apart.

Top Tips: It's easy to get confused between **mitosis** and **meiosis**. Mitosis produces cells for growth and replaces damaged cells. Meiosis is for sexual reproduction and creates gametes.

Cloning Mammals

Q1 Complete each of the statements about **cloning** below by circling the correct words.

a) Cloning is a type of **asexual** / **sexual** reproduction.

b) Cloning produces cells with genes that are genetically **different from** / **identical to** the original cell.

Q2 Draw lines to match each of the '**cloning terms**' below with its meaning.

diploid nucleus	a developing fertilised egg
enucleation	body cell nucleus containing the full number of chromosomes
embryo	removal of the nucleus from a cell

Q3 The diagram shows the **procedure** that can be used to **clone** a sheep.

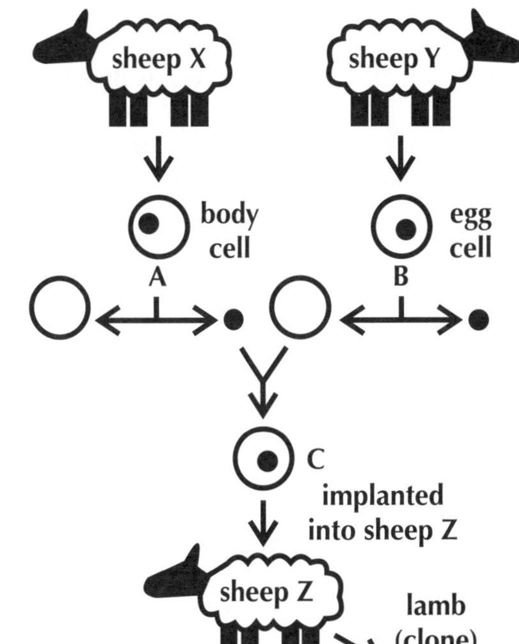

a) Which of the labelled cells in the diagram are genetically identical to each other? Explain your answer.

....

....

....

b) Which of the sheep (X, Y or Z) will the clone be genetically identical to, and why?

....

....

....

c) When the embryo stage is reached in this process, it is possible to divide up the embryo cells, and implant different cells into different surrogates. What would be the effect of doing this?

....

d) In normal sexual reproduction, fertilisation is the fusion of the female and male gametes and their genetic material. Explain the difference between this process and cloning.

....

....

....

Cloning Mammals

Q4 **Cloning** mammals has lots of practical uses.

a) Scientists are creating genetically modified pigs, whose organs are compatible with the human body. Explain why being able to clone these pigs could benefit humans.

....

....

....

b) Circle **two** other reasons why humans might want to clone mammals.

Cloning animals is easy and fast.

Cloning increases the genetic variety of a species.

Studying cloned animals could help us to understand the ageing process.

Cloning could be used to help preserve endangered species.

Q5 Cloning animals has its **disadvantages**.

a) Cloning can lead to a population of animals having a reduced gene pool. Explain why this could cause problems for the animals.

....

....

....

b) Give **two** other problems associated with cloning animals.

....

....

Q6 The first **mammal** to be cloned from an adult body cell was **Dolly the sheep**. She was born in 1996.

Describe how you could clone a mammal, starting with a body cell and an unfertilised egg cell.

....

....

....

....

....

Stem Cells

Q1 Tick the correct boxes to show whether the following statements are **true** or **false**.

		True	False
a)	Cells in an early embryo are unspecialised.	☐	☐
b)	Blood cells are undifferentiated.	☐	☐
c)	Nerve cells are specialised cells.	☐	☐
d)	Adult stem cells are as versatile as embryonic stem cells.	☐	☐
e)	Stem cells in bone marrow can differentiate into any type of cell.	☐	☐
f)	Most animal cells lose the ability to differentiate at an early stage.	☐	☐
g)	Lots of plant cells lose the ability to differentiate at an early stage.	☐	☐

Q2 Scientists in the UK are carrying out research into the use of stem cells in **medicine**.

a) Describe one way in which stem cells are **already** used in medicine.

....

....

b) Describe how it might be possible to use embryonic stem cells to treat disease in the future.

....

....

....

Q3 People have **different opinions** when it comes to embryonic **stem cell research**.

a) Give one argument **in favour** of stem cell research.

....

....

b) Give one argument **against** stem cell research.

....

....

Top Tips: In the future stem cells might be used to cure all sorts of diseases we can't cure now. But to get there we need to do research, and any research that uses embryos is going to be controversial. So it's a good idea to listen to all the arguments on both sides so you can work out what you think.

Mixed Questions — B2 Topic 1

Q1 Your **DNA** carries the **instructions** that tell your cells how to make **proteins**.

a) The sequence of bases in part of one strand of a DNA molecule is as follows:

A–A–T–C–C–A–A–T–C

Write down the **complementary sequence** of bases on the other strand of DNA.

....

b) Name the **two people** who built the first accurate model of the structure of DNA.

....

c) Complete each of the following statements about DNA by circling the correct words.

i) A DNA molecule is made up of **two** / **three** strands of DNA coiled into a **double** / **triple** helix.

ii) The strands are held together by **covalent bonds** / **hydrogen bonds** between pairs of bases.

iii) Adenine always pairs with **thymine** / **cytosine** and guanine always pairs with **thymine** / **cytosine**.

d) A mutation in a rabbit's gene caused one of its proteins to stop working properly.
Explain how a mutation can affect a protein's function like this.

....

....

....

Q2 a) What unique characteristic do **stem cells** have which ordinary body cells don't have?

....

b) Suggest why **embryos** contain many stem cells.

....

....

c) Scientists have experimented with growing stem cells in different conditions.

i) What is the name of the process by which stem cells **divide** for growth?

....

ii) Complete this sentence about the process you named in part **i)** by circling the correct word.

This process makes two cells that are genetically **identical** / **different** to the original cell.

Mixed Questions — B2 Topic 1

Q3 Mosquitoes have **three pairs** of **chromosomes** in their body cells. The diagram below shows a cell from a mosquito which is about to divide by **meiosis**.

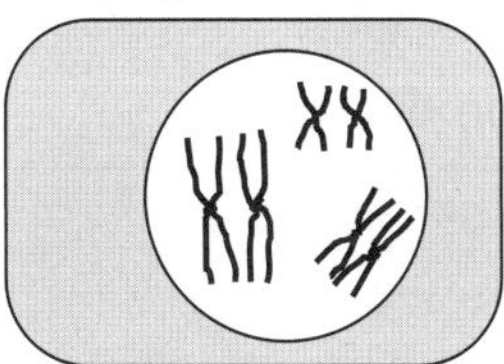

a) Draw the chromosomes in one of the cells produced from this cell:

i) after the first division stage of meiosis.

ii) after the second division stage of meiosis.

b) To draw the diagram, a scientist looked at the mosquito cell under a light microscope. The actual cell is **0.001 cm** wide. The image of the cell is **0.8 cm** wide. Calculate the magnification of the image.

....

....

Q4 **Proteins** are large molecules coded for by **DNA**.

a) Explain how each of the following are involved in building **new proteins**.

i) Genes ....

ii) Amino acids ....

iii) Codons ....

iv) mRNA ....

v) Ribosomes ....

b) Some **human diseases** are caused by a **lack** of a **working protein**, e.g. people with type 1 diabetes don't produce enough of the protein insulin or don't produce any at all. Briefly describe how bacteria can be genetically modified to make human insulin.

....

....

....

Respiration

Q1 Part of the **word equation** for one type of **respiration** is shown below.

a) Complete the equation for respiration.

.... + oxygen → carbon dioxide + ... (+ ....)

b) What type of respiration is this? ....

Q2 Which of these statements is **not** true of respiration? Underline the correct answer.

It is a process used by all living organisms.

It releases energy from food.

It is another word for breathing.

It can be aerobic or anaerobic.

Q3 Give **three** things that the body uses the **energy** obtained in respiration for.

....

....

Q4 Draw lines to match the **body part** or **process** to the correct description.

capillaries	The system that provides the food source needed for respiration.
circulatory system	The movement of particles from areas of higher concentration to areas of lower concentration.
diffusion	The smallest blood vessels that carry blood to all body cells.
digestive system	The system that carries substances like glucose, oxygen and carbon dioxide around your body.

Q5 The diagram shows **blood** passing through **muscle tissue**.

a) On the diagram, draw labelled arrows to show whether **oxygen (O_2)**, **glucose (G)** and **carbon dioxide (CO_2)** move **into** or **out of** the muscle cells.

b) Explain how these substances move into and out of the blood in terms of concentration.

....

....

....

Respiration and Exercise

Q1 Humans can respire **aerobically** — if there isn't enough oxygen available we can also respire **anaerobically**.

a) Give **one** disadvantage of anaerobic respiration compared to aerobic respiration.

....

....

b) In what circumstances would a human start respiring anaerobically?

....

....

c) Write the **word equation** for anaerobic respiration in humans.

.... → .... (+ ....)

Q2 Joe investigated how **exercise** affects his **heart rate**. He took his **pulse** after **sitting still** for five minutes, after **walking** for five minutes and after **running** for five minutes. Joe's results are shown on the graph on the right.

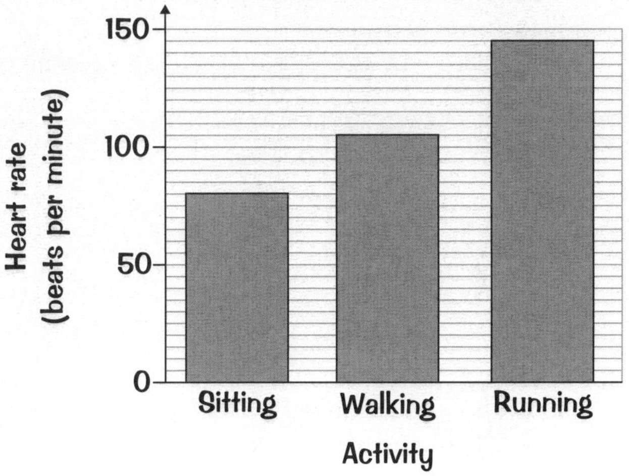

a) How many beats per minute did running increase Joe's heart rate by, compared to sitting still?

....

b) Explain why running increases Joe's heart rate more than walking does.

....

....

....

....

c) Joe has a **stroke volume** of 65 cm^3. Calculate Joe's **cardiac output**, in cm^3 per minute, when he is **sitting still**.

cardiac output = heart rate × stroke volume

....

....

Respiration and Exercise

Q3 Jim is a keen runner. He takes part in a 400 metre race. The **graph** below shows Jim's **breathing rate** before, during and after the race.

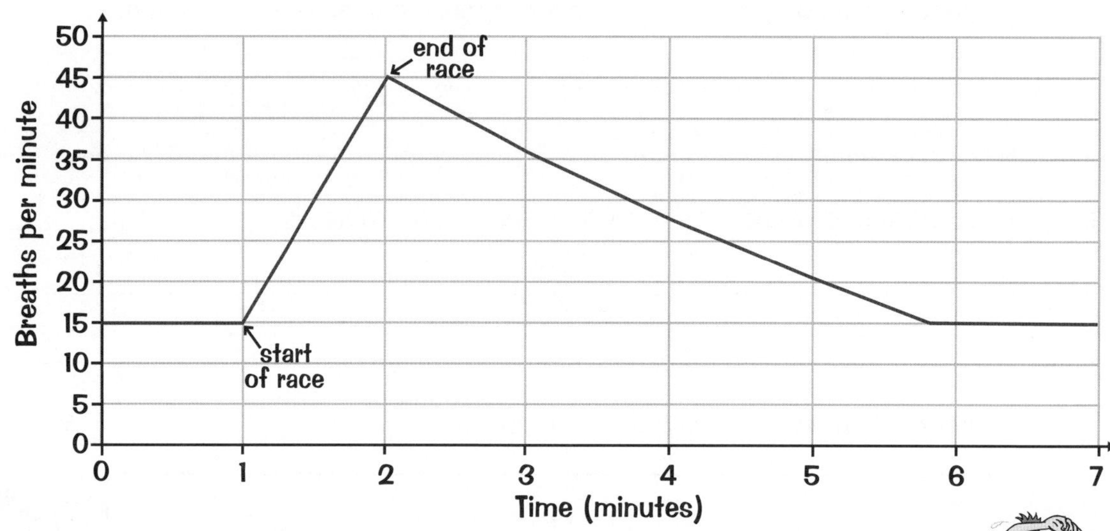

a) How much does Jim's breathing rate go up during the race?

.... **breaths per minute**

b) Explain why exercise makes Jim's breathing rate increase.

....

....

....

....

c) As he gets to the end of the race, Jim's muscles start to hurt. Explain why his muscles feel painful.

....

....

....

d) Explain why Jim's breathing rate **doesn't** return to normal immediately after the race. Use the term '**EPOC**' in your answer.

EPOC stands for 'excess post-exercise oxygen consumption'.

....

....

....

....

Photosynthesis

Q1 Circle the correct word(s) in each pair to complete the passage below.

> Stomata are tiny holes found on the surface of the leaf that are used for **mineral uptake / gas exchange**. They allow carbon dioxide to diffuse **in / out** and oxygen to diffuse **in / out** of the leaf during photosynthesis. The stomata also allow water vapour to **leave / enter** the leaf — this water **loss / gain** is called **transcription / transpiration**.

Q2 **Photosynthesis** is the process that produces 'food' in plants. Use some of the words from the box below to complete the equation for photosynthesis.

oxygen **carbon dioxide** **nitrogen** **water** **glucose** **sodium chloride**

.... + ... $\xrightarrow[\text{chlorophyll}]{\text{sunlight}}$ .... + ...

Q3 Tick the boxes to show whether the following statements are **true** or **false**.

		True	False
a)	Photosynthesis happens inside the chloroplasts.	☐	☐
b)	Photosynthesis happens in all plant cells.	☐	☐
c)	Plants absorb carbon dioxide from the air.	☐	☐
d)	Plant cells don't respire.	☐	☐
e)	Sunlight provides the energy for photosynthesis.	☐	☐

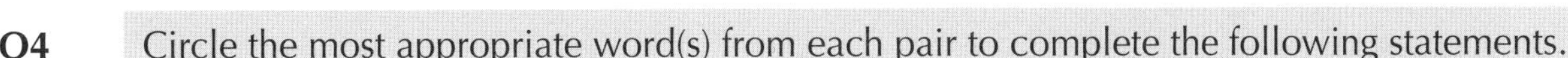

Q4 Circle the most appropriate word(s) from each pair to complete the following statements.

a) The rate of photosynthesis depends on the availability of **raw materials / products**.

b) When photosynthesis is taking place **quickly / slowly**, more oxygen gas is being produced.

c) You can measure the rate of photosynthesis by counting the bubbles of **oxygen / carbon dioxide** produced by some pondweed in a given time.

Top Tips: Photosynthesis is one of those ideas that's absolutely central to biology. After all, if green plants couldn't trap the sun's energy, that would pretty much be the end of life on Earth — and certainly of us. So why not go and hug a tree now to say thanks. Or at least be kind to a pot plant...

Photosynthesis

Q5 A diagram of a leaf in cross-section is shown below.

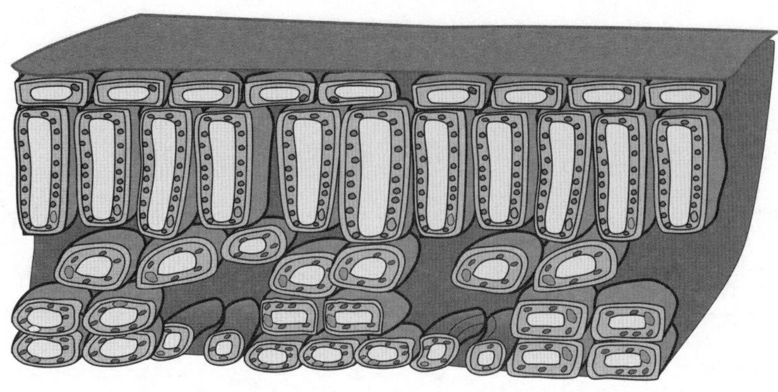

Suggest how each of the following features of the leaf are important for photosynthesis:

a) The leaf has a **broad surface**.

....

....

b) The leaf is **green**.

....

....

Q6 Below are some straightforward questions about **limiting factors**. Hooray.

a) Explain the meaning of the term "limiting factor".

....

b) List **three** things that can limit the rate of photosynthesis.

1. ....

2. ....

3. ....

c) The limiting factor at a particular time depends on the environmental conditions, e.g. season (such as winter). Name **two** other environmental conditions that may affect the rate of photosynthesis.

1. ....

2. ....

The Rate of Photosynthesis

Q1 Lucy investigated the **volume of oxygen** produced by pondweed at **different intensities of light**. Her results are shown in the table below.

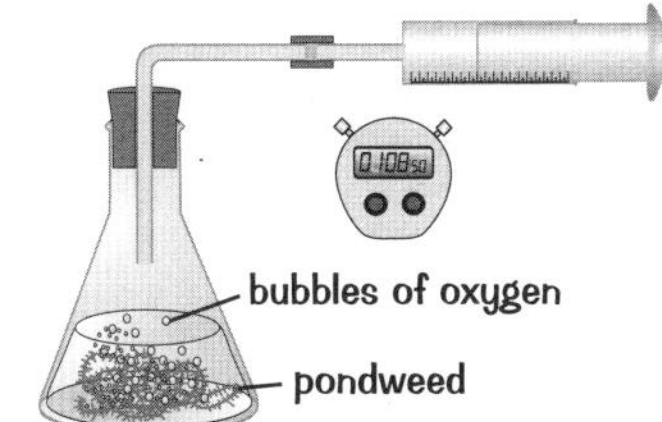

Relative light intensity	1	2	3	4	5
Vol. of O_2 produced in 10 mins (ml)	12	25	13	48	61

a) Plot a graph of her results.

b) **i)** One of Lucy's results is probably wrong. Circle this point on the graph.

ii) Suggest what error Lucy might have made when she collected this result.

....

....

....

c) Describe the relationship shown on the graph between light intensity and photosynthesis rate.

....

....

d) Would you expect this relationship to continue if Lucy continued to increase the light intensity? Explain your answer.

....

....

Q2 Farmer Fred doesn't put his cows out during the winter because the grass is not growing.

a) State **two** differences between summer and winter conditions that affect the rate of photosynthesis in the grass.

1. ....

2. ....

b) How are the rate of photosynthesis and the growth rate of grass related?

....

....

The Rate of Photosynthesis

Q3 Seth investigated the effect of different concentrations of **carbon dioxide** on the rate of photosynthesis of his Swiss cheese plant. The results are shown on the graph below.

rate of photosynthesis

light intensity

— 0.4% CO_2
— 0.1% CO_2
— 0.04% CO_2

a) What effect does increasing the concentration of CO_2 have on the rate of photosynthesis?

b) Explain why all the graphs level off eventually.

Q4 Average **daytime summer temperatures** in different habitats around the world are shown in the table below.

Habitat	Temperature (°C)
Forest	19
Arctic	0
Desert	32
Grassland	22
Rainforest	27

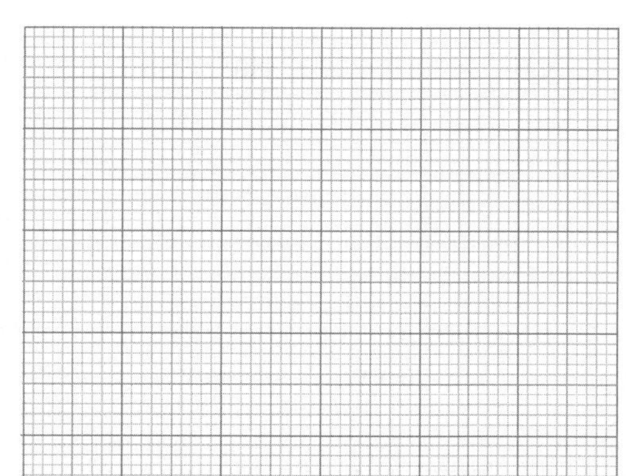

a) Plot a **bar chart** for these results on the grid.

b) From the values for temperature, in which area would you expect fewest plants to grow?

c) Suggest a reason for your answer above using the terms **enzymes** and **photosynthesis**.

d) **Explain** why very few plants can usually grow in the desert even though it has a much higher average temperature than the rainforest where many varieties of plants can grow.

Osmosis

Q1 This diagram shows a tank separated into two by a partially permeable membrane.

a) On which side of the membrane is there the higher concentration of water molecules?

....

b) In which direction would you expect **more** water molecules to travel — from A to B or from B to A?

....

c) Predict whether the level of liquid on side B will **rise** or **fall**. Explain your answer.

The liquid level on side B will ...., because ....

....

Q2 Some **potato cylinders** were placed in solutions of different **salt concentrations**. At the start of the experiment each cylinder was 50 mm long. Their final lengths are recorded in the table below.

Concentration of salt (molar)	Final length of potato cylinder (mm)	Change in length of potato cylinder (mm)
0	60	
0.25	58	
0.5	56	
0.75	70	
1	50	
1.25	45	

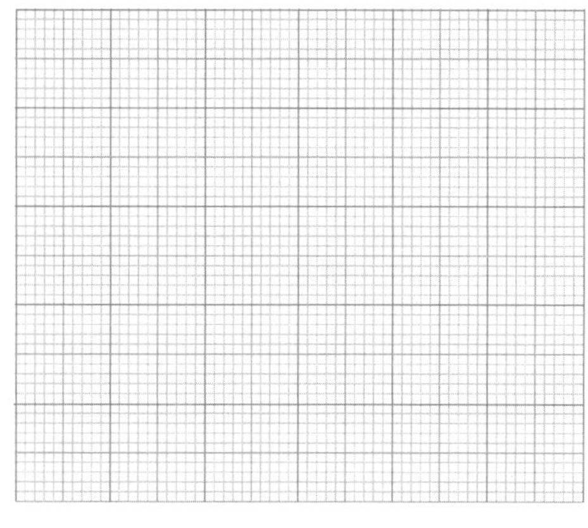

a) Plot the points for concentration of salt solution vs final length of potato cylinders on the grid.

b) Work out the change in length of each of the cylinders and complete the table above.

c) Study the pattern of the results.

i) State the salt concentration(s) that produced unexpected results. ....

ii) Suggest a method for deciding which of the results are correct.

....

d) State **three** factors that should have been kept constant to ensure this was a fair test.

....

....

Water Uptake and Loss in Plants

Q1 Flowering plants have **tube networks** for moving substances around.

a) Name the vessels that carry **sugars** around the plant. ....

b) Circle the correct word from each pair to complete the following sentence.

> Sugars are made in the **roots** / **leaves** and transported to parts of the plant that are **growing** / **dying** and to the plant's **storage** / **protective** tissues.

Q2 Choose from the following words to complete the passage.
Each word should only be used once, or not at all.

osmosis **leaves** **evaporation** **roots** **flowers**
phloem **diffusion** **transpiration** **xylem**

> Most water leaves plants through the .... by the processes of .... and .... This creates a slight shortage of water in the leaf, which draws water from the rest of the plant through the .... vessels. This causes more water to be drawn up from the .... This whole process is called ....

Q3 A diagram of a **cell** found in the **root** of a **plant** is shown on the right.

a) Name the type of cell shown. ....

b) Why does this type of cell have the particular shape shown?

....

c) Explain why water moves into the plant's roots from the soil.

....

....

d) Explain how these specialised cells absorb mineral ions from the soil.
Use the words **active transport**, **concentration**, **respiration** and **energy** in your answer.

....

....

Top Tips: Water transport is the name of the game here — this stuff is all about how a plant keeps a steady stream of water moving from its roots, up its stem and into its leaves.

Distribution of Organisms

Q1 Tick the boxes to show whether the following statements are **true** or **false**.

		True	False
a)	A habitat is the place where an organism lives.	☐	☐
b)	The distribution of an organism is how an organism interacts with its habitat.	☐	☐
c)	To study the distribution of an organism you can measure how common it is in two sample areas and compare them.	☐	☐

Q2 Circle the correct word from each pair to complete the following statements.

a) You would use a pitfall trap to investigate the distribution of **ground insects** / **pond animals**.

b) The top of a pitfall trap is **completely covered** / **partly open**.

c) The sides of a pitfall trap are **steep** / **shallow** so that insects that fall into it **can** / **can't** get out again.

Q3 Sally sampled the population of **water snails** in two ponds.

a) Name a piece of equipment that Sally might have used to collect the snails.

....

b) Sally sampled each pond **three** times. The table below shows her results.
Complete the table by filling in the missing numbers.

	Sample 1	Sample 2	Sample 3	Mean number of snails
Pond 1	2 snails	6 snails	7 snails	
Pond 2	10 snails	9 snails		11 snails

Q4 Mark wants to compare the distribution of beetles in two different areas.
He decides to collect the beetles using a **pooter**.

a) Briefly describe how to collect an insect using a pooter.

....

....

b) Explain how Mark could use a pooter to compare the distribution of beetles in the two areas.

....

....

c) Name **two** things Mark needs to keep the same both times to make sure his test is fair.

1. .... 2. ....

More on the Distribution of Organisms

Q1 **Environmental factors** can affect how organisms are **distributed**.

a) **Light intensity** is an environmental factor. Name a device you could use to measure light intensity.

....

b) i) Name **one** other environmental factor that can affect the distribution of organisms.

....

ii) Name a piece of equipment that you could use to measure this factor.

....

Q2 Some students wanted to estimate the size of the population of **clover plants** around their school. To do this, they use the piece of equipment shown on the right.

1 m

1 m

a) What is this piece of equipment called?

....

b) The school field is 250 m long by 180 m wide. Hannah counted 11 clover plants in a 1 m^2 area of the field. **Approximately** how many clover plants are there likely to be on the whole field?

....

....

c) Lisa decided to collect data from five different 1 m^2 areas of the school field. Her results are shown in the table below.

	Area 1	Area 2	Area 3	Area 4	Area 5
No. of plants	11	9	8	9	7

i) What was the **average** number of clover plants per m^2 in Lisa's survey?

....

ii) Use Lisa's data to estimate the population size of clover plants on the field.

....

d) Whose estimation of population size is likely to be more accurate? Explain your answer.

....

....

Top Tips: Some questions may feel like you're doing maths rather than biology... but you can't get away from things like averages — you do need to know how to work them out for the exam. Booo.

Mixed Questions — B2 Topic 2

Q1 Humans can respire **aerobically** and **anaerobically**.

a) Give a definition of respiration, including where it happens in the body.

....

....

b) Complete the following sentences about anaerobic respiration in humans.

Anaerobic respiration is respiration without ....

A waste product, ..., is produced. ....

energy is released during anaerobic respiration than during aerobic respiration.

c) Anaerobic respiration is not as efficient as aerobic respiration. Why is it still useful to us?

....

....

Q2 The diagram shows a **plant**, A, growing in a **tropical rainforest**.

plant A

a) Which factor is most likely to limit the rate of photosynthesis in plant A? Explain your answer.

....

....

b) Give **two** other factors that often limit the rate of photosynthesis in plants.

....

c) Plant A needs to take in water to keep photosynthesising.

i) Give the name of the vessels that carry water from the plant's roots to its leaves.

....

ii) Explain how the **transpiration stream** helps to keep the leaves supplied with water.

....

....

....

Mixed Questions — B2 Topic 2

Q3 A student was given **three solutions** labelled X, Y and Z. He set up the experiment shown on the right and left it for a day. At the end of the experiment, the water outside the membrane contained particles X and Y, but not Z.

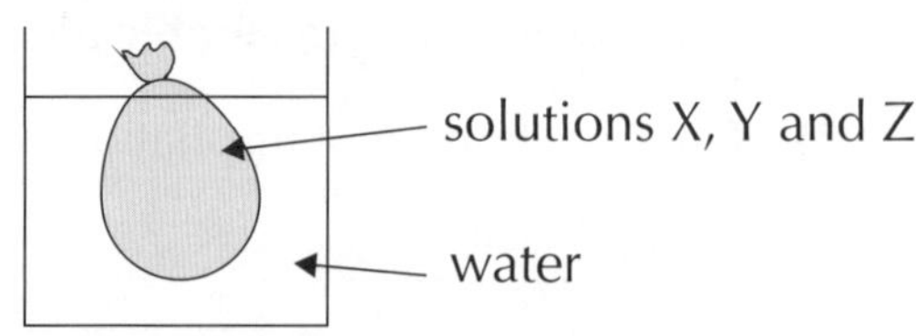

a) Name the process by which particles of X and Y moved through the membrane.

....

b) What can you conclude about the relative sizes of the X, Y and Z particles?

....

c) X, Y and Z were solutions of amino acid, protein and glucose. Which of these solutions was Z?

....

d) During the experiment, some water particles moved from the beaker into the membrane. Name the process the water particles moved by. ....

Q4 Eve and Bill work together to study the **distribution** of **harebells** in a meadow. They each pick a **sample area** and use a **quadrat** to estimate the population size.

Harebells are pretty little blue flowers.

a) Define the term 'distribution'.

....

b) Explain how you can use a **1 m² quadrat** to find the **mean number** of harebells **per m²** in an area.

....

....

....

c) The results of Bill and Eve's investigation are shown in the table on the right.

i) Fill in the gaps in the results table.

	Number of harebells				
	Quadrat 1	Quadrat 2	Quadrat 3	Quadrat 4	Mean
Bill's area	5	7	2	4	
Eve's Area	8	11		12	10

ii) Eve has read that harebells grow best in **acidic soil**. She wonders if that's why there are more harebells in her area. Suggest how Eve could test this hypothesis.

....

....

d) Bill's friend Ben is studying the number of **spiders** in the meadow. The meadow is covered in **long grass**. Name a piece of equipment that Ben could use to collect spiders in the meadow.

....

Evidence For Evolution

Q1 Fossils were found in this sample of **rock**.

Fossil A
Fossil B

a) Explain what a fossil is.

....

....

b) Name **two** things that a fossil can tell us about an ancient organism.

1. ....

2. ....

c) Explain why scientists think that fossil B in the picture above is **older** than fossil A.

....

....

Q2 The fossil record is **incomplete** — there are gaps in it.
Give **three reasons** why we do not have fossils of some organisms.

1. ....

2. ....

3. ....

Q3 Tim is looking at the two pictures on the right. They show the **bones** in a **human hand** and a **bat's wing**.

Human hand

Bat's wing

a) Give the name for a limb that has **five digits**.

....

b) Tim says "Humans look quite different from bats, so I think they evolved from different ancestors."
Is Tim likely to be correct? Explain your answer.

....

....

....

Growth and Development

Q1 If an organism increases in size or mass, it is **growing**.

a) Give **one** way to measure the **size** of an organism.

....

b) How do you measure the **dry mass** of an organism?

....

Q2 Animals and plants **grow** in different ways.

a) Draw lines to match each of the **growth processes** below to its correct definition.

CELL ELONGATION	When one cell splits into two by mitosis.
CELL DIFFERENTIATION	Where a cell expands, making the cell bigger.
CELL DIVISION	The process by which a cell changes to become specialised for its job.

b) Give **one** difference in growth between plants and animals.

....

....

Q3 A baby's growth was recorded. The results are shown on the **growth chart** on the right.

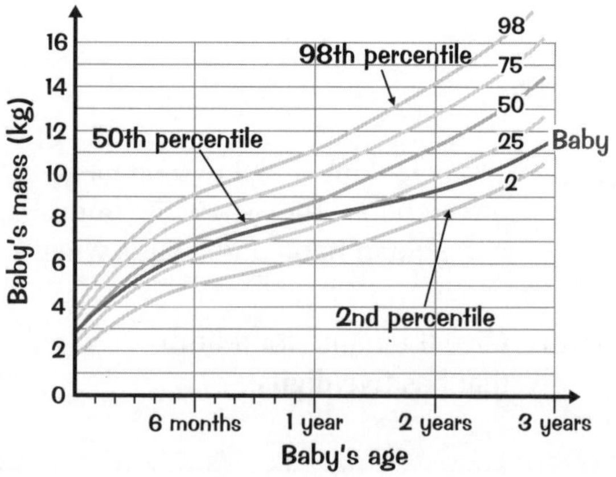

a) Explain what a growth chart is used for.

....

....

....

b) The baby's growth was above the 25th percentile at 6 months. Explain what the 25th percentile shows.

....

c) Would a doctor be concerned about the mass of this baby at 3 years? Explain your answer.

....

....

Cell Organisation and the Circulatory System

Q1 Complete the passage below using some of the words from the box.

function tissue organ tissues organs cells system circulatory

A .... (e.g. muscle) is a group of similar .... that work together to carry out a particular function. An .... (e.g. the heart) is a group of different .... that work together to perform a particular function. An organ system (e.g. the .... system) is a group of .... working together to perform a particular function.

Q2 Sort the following list by writing each term in the correct place in the table below.

sperm blood digestive system tree liver
muscle excretory system white blood cell leaf cat

Cell	Tissue	Organ	Organ system	Organism

Q3 The diagram below shows the human **heart**, as seen from the front. The left atrium has been labelled for you. Complete the remaining labels **a)** to **h)**.

a) ....

b) ....

c) ....

d) ....

e) ....

f) ....

left atrium

g) ....

h) ....

Q4 Tick the boxes to say whether each statement below is **true** or **false**.

		True	False
a)	Arteries always carry oxygenated blood.	☐	☐
b)	The atria of the heart have thicker walls than the ventricles.	☐	☐
c)	The right side of the heart pumps deoxygenated blood.	☐	☐
d)	Valves prevent blood flowing backwards.	☐	☐

The Circulatory System — The Blood

Q1 Which of these statements are **true** and which are **false**? Tick the correct boxes.

		True	False
a)	The main function of red blood cells is to fight germs.	☐	☐
b)	A higher than normal white blood cell count means you're more likely to get an infection.	☐	☐
c)	Glucose can be found in the blood.	☐	☐
d)	The liquid part of blood is called urea.	☐	☐
e)	Platelets seal wounds to prevent blood loss.	☐	☐

Q2 **Red blood cells** carry **oxygen** in the blood.

a) i) Name the substance in these cells that combines with oxygen. ....

ii) Name the substance created when oxygen joins with this substance. ....

b) Red blood cells are replaced roughly every 120 days.
Approximately how many times per year are all the red blood cells in the body replaced?

....

Q3 **White blood cells** defend the body against **disease**.

a) State three ways in which white blood cells can protect your body from microorganisms.

1. ....

2. ....

3. ....

b) A man was feeling unwell and went to see his doctor. The doctor did a blood test and found that the patient's white blood cell count was higher than normal. Suggest a reason for this.

....

Q4 **Plasma** is the substance that carries everything in the blood.

a) List **six** substances that are carried by **plasma**.

....

....

b) For each of the substances listed in the table, state where in the body it is travelling **from** and **to**.

Substance	Travelling from	Travelling to
Urea		
Carbon dioxide		
Glucose		

The Circulatory System — Blood Vessels

Q1 Draw lines to match each of the words below with its correct description.

artery	hole in the middle of a tube
capillary	microscopic blood vessel
lumen	vessel that takes blood towards the heart
vein	vessel that takes blood away from the heart

Q2 Circle the correct word in each of the sentences below.

a) **Arteries** / **Veins** contain valves to prevent the blood going backwards.

b) **Capillaries** / **Veins** have walls that are permeable.

c) **Arteries** / **Capillaries** have smooth muscle in their walls.

d) The blood pressure in the **arteries** / **veins** is higher than in the **arteries** / **veins**.

Q3 Gareth did an experiment to compare the elasticity of **arteries** and **veins**. He dissected out an artery and a vein from a piece of fresh meat. He then took a 5 cm length of each vessel, hung different masses on it, and measured how much it stretched. His results are shown in the table.

a) Suggest **one** way that Gareth could tell which was the artery and which was the vein when he was dissecting the meat.

....

....

mass added (g)	length of blood vessel (mm)	
	artery	vein
0	50	50
5	51	53
10	53	56
15	55	59
20	56	-

b) If Gareth plots his results on a graph, which variable should he put on the vertical axis, and why?

....

c) Which vessel stretched more easily? Explain why this was.

....

d) Why did he take both vessels from the same piece of meat?

....

Top Tips: It really important to remember the differences between arteries, veins and capillaries — don't get them mixed up. It's the kind of thing that crops up on exams all the time...

The Digestive System and Enzymes

Q1 Fill in the boxes to label this diagram of the human **digestive system**.

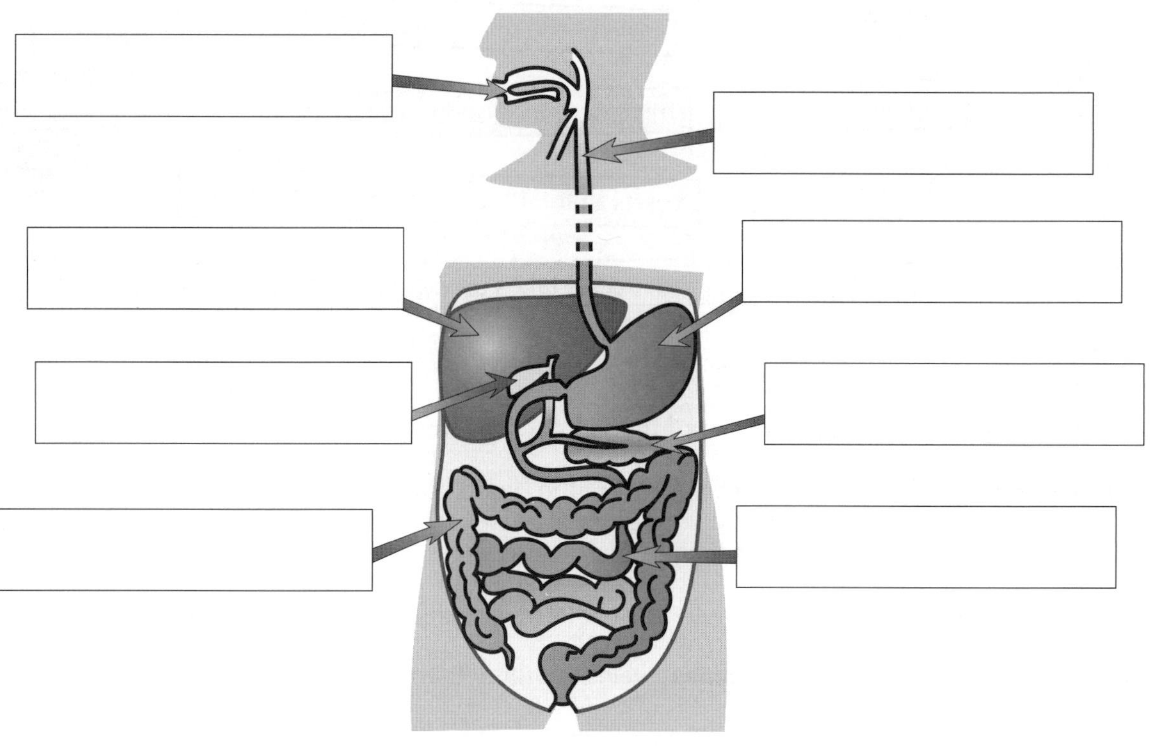

Q2 Number the boxes 1 to 4 to show the **order** that food passes through these parts of the **digestive system**.

- ☐ stomach
- ☐ mouth
- ☐ large intestine
- ☐ small intestine

Q3 During digestion, **enzymes** break **large molecules** down into **smaller molecules** that can be absorbed by the body.

a) Look at the list below. **Underline** all the large molecules. **Circle** all the small molecules.

amino acids sugars proteins fatty acids
fats glycerol starch

b) Name one example of a **carbohydrase** enzyme. ....

c) State what type of enzyme **pepsin** is. ....

The Digestive System and Enzymes

Q4 Choose from the words below to complete the table showing where **amylase**, **protease**, **lipase** and **bile** are made. You may use some words more than once and you might not need some of them.

pancreas | liver | salivary glands | small intestine | large intestine | stomach | gall bladder | kidneys

Amylase	Protease	Lipase	Bile

Q5 Describe the **role** of each of the following in digestion:

a) Oesophagus ....

b) Gall bladder ....

c) Pancreas ....

d) Liver ....

e) Large intestine..........

Q6 Fill in the boxes to show how the **three main food groups** are **broken down** during digestion.

a)

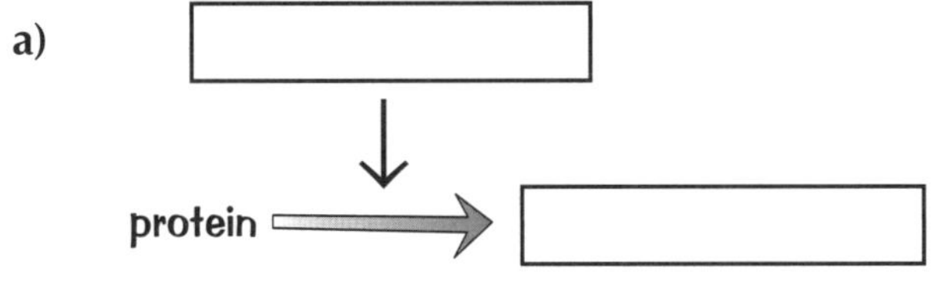

b)

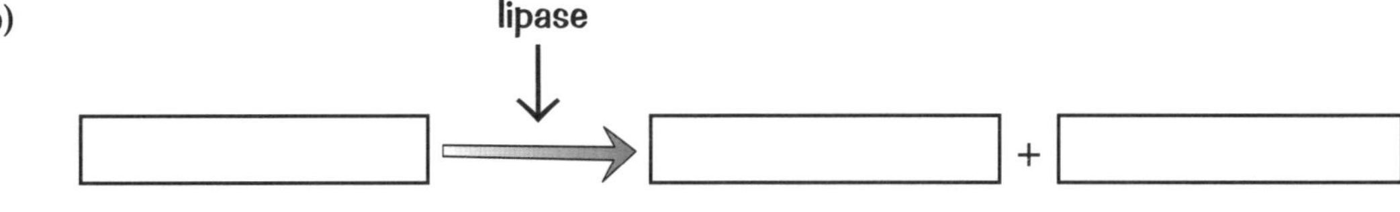

c)

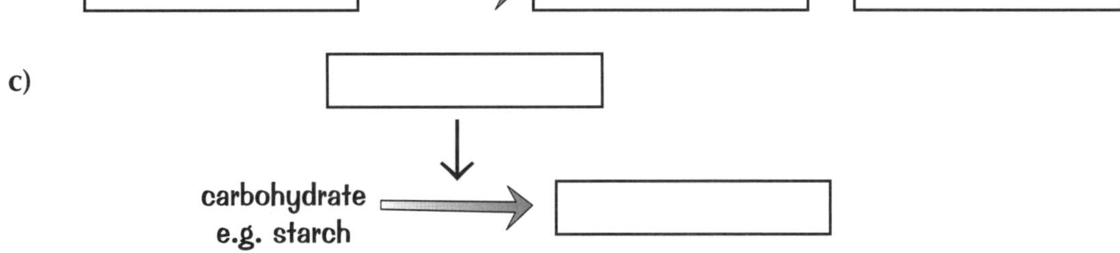

Top Tips: The stuff on digestion shouldn't take you too long to learn. The trickiest bits are probably all those enzyme names and what they do — so make sure you've got it all clear in your head.

Investigating Digestive Enzymes

Q1 Jenny investigated how the concentration of an enzyme affects the rate of digestion. She filled three pieces of visking tubing with **starch** solution and different concentrations of the enzyme **amylase**.

a) Explain why **visking tubing** is often used as a model for the gut.

....

....

b) Jenny put the pieces of visking tubing into three test tubes filled with distilled water, like this:

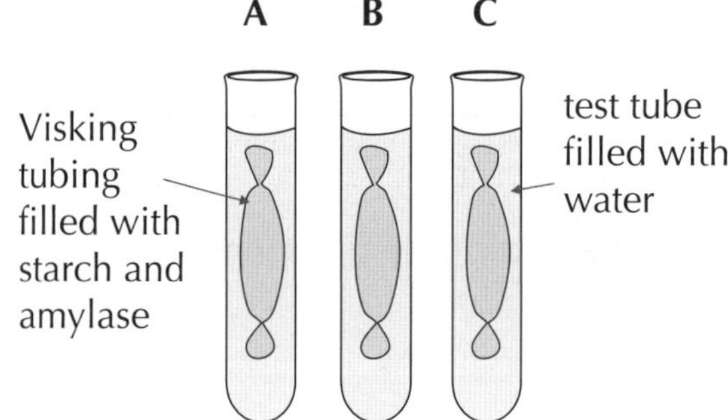

After four hours she tested the water outside each piece of tubing with Benedict's reagent. Her results are shown in the table below.

Tube	Amylase concentration	Colour of Benedict's reagent
A	5 mol/dm^3	brick-red
B	0.5 mol/dm^3	yellow
C	2 mol/dm^3	orange

i) Name the substance that Benedict's reagent is used as a test for. ....

ii) State the colour of Benedict's reagent when none of this substance is present.

....

c) Explain what the results of Jenny's experiment tell you about how enzyme concentration affects the rate of reaction.

....

....

....

d) Jenny tried the experiment again using a very high concentration of amylase. This time the reaction didn't happen any faster than the reaction in tube A. Explain this result.

....

....

More on Digestion

Q1 a) Circle the correct words from each pair to complete this passage about **bile**.

Bile is stored in the **gall bladder** / **pancreas** before being released into the **liver** / **small intestine**. Bile **acidifies** / **neutralises** the material from the stomach which provides the optimum pH for the **enzymes** / **microorganisms** in the rest of the digestive system to work. Bile breaks **fat** / **glycerol** into smaller droplets.

b) Explain how emulsification helps digestion.

....

....

Finest emulsion

Q2 **Peristalsis** helps the food that we eat get to the stomach from the mouth.

a) Explain what **peristalsis** is.

....

....

b) The diagram below shows peristalsis happening in the alimentary canal.

i) Label the **longitudinal** muscles.

ii) Label the **circular** muscles.

iii) Add an arrow to the diagram to show which way the food is travelling.

food

c) Briefly explain how peristalsis works.

....

....

....

More on Digestion

Q3 The inside of the **small intestine** is covered in millions of **villi**.

a) Villi have a **single layer** of surface cells. Explain how this feature helps to speed up digestion.

....

b) Give **one** other way that the villi are adapted to make digestion more efficient.
Explain how the feature you have named helps to speed up digestion.

Feature: ....

Explanation: ....

....

Q4 Pablo conducted an experiment to investigate the effect of surface area on the uptake of nutrients, using four **gelatine cubes** of **different sizes**. He placed the cubes in a dish of food dye and measured how quickly they absorbed the dye.

Pablo's results are shown in the table below.

Size (cm)	Surface area (cm^2)	Time taken for dye uptake (s)
1 x 1 x 1		41.6
2 x 2 x 2		9.3
5 x 5 x 5		1.7
10 x 10 x 10		0.4

a) Calculate the missing values for **surface area**.

b) Complete these statements by circling the correct word.

i) As the cubes become bigger in size their surface area becomes **bigger** / **smaller**.

ii) As the surface area becomes bigger the rate of dye uptake **increases** / **decreases**.

c) Explain how the results from this experiment show that villi increase the rate of nutrient uptake from the gut.

....

....

....

Functional Foods

Q1 Explain what is meant by the term '**functional food**'.

....

....

Q2 **Probiotics** are added to some foods.

a) What are **probiotics**?

....

....

b) Name **one** example of a type of bacteria that is used in probiotic foods.

....

c) Circle **two** examples of common probiotic foods from the list below.

pasta soya milk yoghurts

vegetables ham

Q3 Some people take **prebiotic** supplements.

a) What are **prebiotics**?

....

b) Suggest what health benefits a person might expect to get from taking a prebiotic supplement.

....

....

....

c) Give **two** natural sources of prebiotics.

1. ....

2. ....

Top Tips: Some bacteria are 'bad' and can cause disease but there are also 'good' bacteria. Everyone has 'good' bacteria in their guts — they're really important for digestion. Some functional foods are designed to try to help the 'good' bacteria to grow and thrive. How very kind of them...

Functional Foods

Q4 Two reports were published about eating **probiotic yoghurts**.

Report A was a magazine article published by the manufacturers of 'Well-U' probiotic yoghurt. It was about two ordinary women who ate two 'Well-U' yoghurts every day for a week.

Report B appeared in a journal. It was a study in which a trial group of 500 hospital patients were given a probiotic yoghurt for breakfast every day. A control group were given normal yoghurt.

Which of these reports has used a more reliable method for investigating probiotic yoghurts? Explain your answer.

....

....

....

Q5 Scientists did an experiment into the effectiveness of **stanol esters** in lowering people's **blood cholesterol**. They asked two groups of 100 people each to use a special spread instead of butter. Group A's spread was based on vegetable oil. Group B's spread was exactly the same, except that it contained large amounts of stanol esters. The cholesterol levels of each group were measured before the start of the experiment, and again after six months. The results are shown in the table.

	Group A / units	Group B / units
Mean blood cholesterol at start	6.3	6.4
Mean blood cholesterol after 6 mths	6.1	5.5

a) Explain the purpose of Group A.

....

b) Why did the scientists use 100 people in each group?

....

c) What precautions should the scientists have taken when choosing people for this experiment, to make sure that their results were valid?

....

d) Why is it necessary to measure the blood cholesterol before the experiment as well as at the end?

....

e) Explain why it is important that people with high blood cholesterol take steps to lower it.

....

Mixed Questions — B2 Topic 3

Q1 **Growth** can involve cells **dividing**, **elongating** or **differentiating**.

a) Describe how plant growth differs from animal growth regarding:

i) cell elongation ....

....

ii) cell division ....

....

iii) cell differentiation ....

....

b) Cells differentiate to become specialised cells, which form **tissues**. Describe what a **tissue** is.

....

....

Q2 The **blood** is a huge **transport system**.

a) **i)** Give the name of the blood cell shown on the right.

....

ii) What is the function of this cell?

....

b) The cell on the right transports oxygen to all parts of the body. Give **two** ways in which this cell is adapted to perform its job. Briefly explain how each adaptation allows it to do its job well.

....

....

....

c) **Capillaries** carry the blood to cells, where oxygen and food can diffuse in, and waste substances can diffuse out. Explain how the capillaries are adapted to suit this function.

....

....

....

Mixed Questions — B2 Topic 3

Q3 The diagram shows part of the **circulatory system**.

Lungs
W
Y
X
Z
Body

a) Name the blood vessels labelled W, X, Y and Z.

W ....

X ....

Y ....

Z ....

b) State one difference in composition between the blood entering the heart from the vena cava and the blood leaving the heart through the aorta.

....

c) Explain how the structure of an artery is adapted for its function.

....

....

d) **i)** Which type of blood vessel contains valves? ....

ii) What is the function of these valves?

....

Q4 During the **digestive process**, **fats** are broken down into fatty acids and glycerol.

a) Which enzyme is responsible for the digestion of fats?

....

b) **Bile** is also involved in the digestion of fats. Describe what bile does to fats.

....

c) **i)** Describe the roles that the **mouth** plays in the digestive process.

....

....

ii) Describe the roles that the **stomach** plays in the digestive process.

....

....

....

The Kidneys

Q1 One of the main roles of the **kidneys** is to remove **urea** from the blood.

a) Urea is a waste product that builds up in the blood as a result of cell metabolism. Name **one** other waste product of cell metabolism.

....

b) Tick the boxes to show whether the following statements about urea are **true** or **false**.

i) The kidneys make urea.

ii) Breaking down excess fats produces urea.

iii) The liver makes urea.

iv) The kidneys remove urea from the bloodstream.

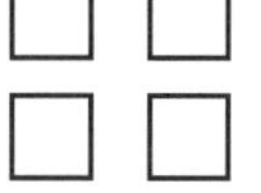

Billy the kid-ney bean

Q2 Fill in the labels on the diagram of the **urinary system** shown below. One of the labels has been done for you.

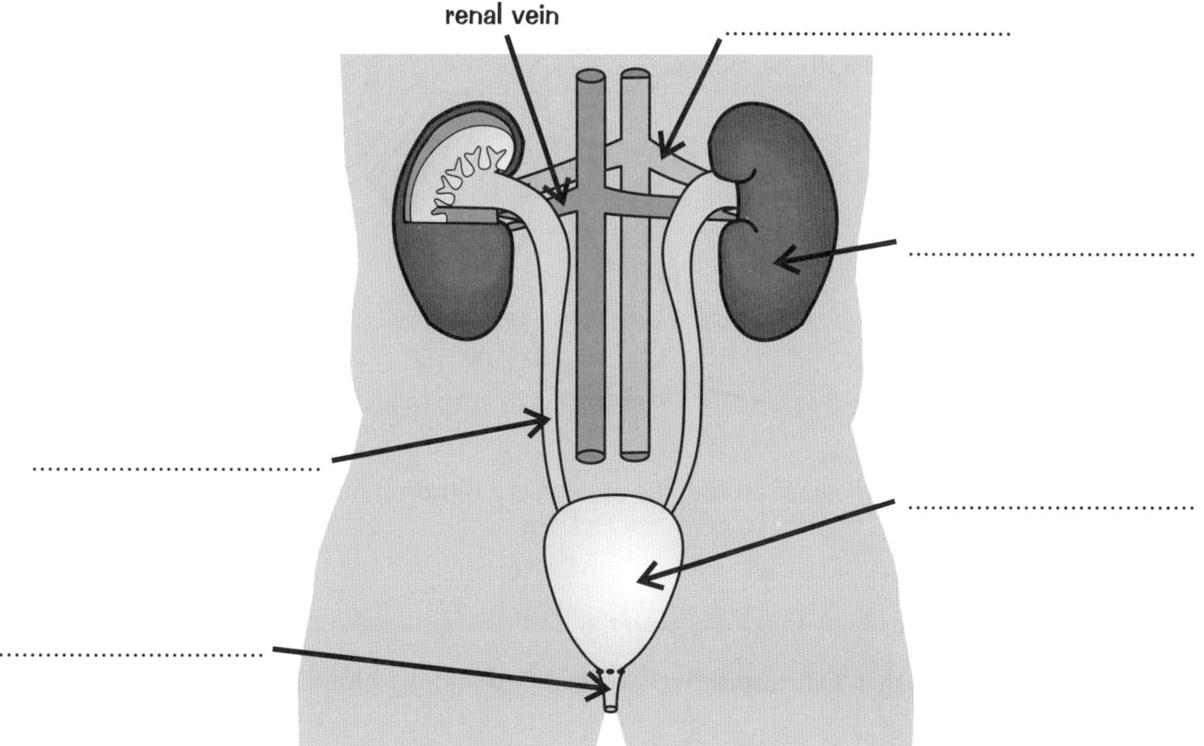

Top Tips: Your kidneys do an ace job of filtering your blood and taking out all the stuff that you don't want or don't need any more. Without them you'd be in all sorts of trouble pretty quickly...

The Kidneys

Q3 The diagram shows the steps that occur from the **entry** to the **exit** of blood in the kidneys. Write the labels **A** to **E** in the diagram to show the correct order. The first one has been done for you.

A Wastes, such as urea, are carried out of the nephron to the bladder.

B A high pressure is built up which squeezes small molecules out of the blood and into the Bowman's capsule.

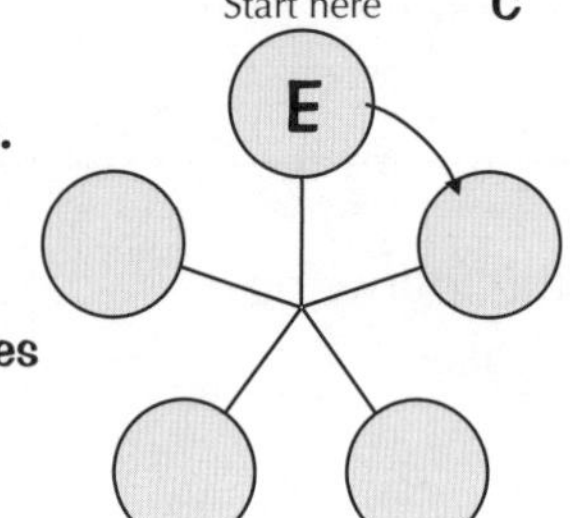

C Useful products are reabsorbed from the nephron and enter the capillaries.

D Molecules travel from the Bowman's capsule along the nephron.

E Blood enters the kidney through the renal artery.

Q4 a) Use the words provided to fill in the missing labels on the diagram of a **nephron** shown below.

first convoluted tubule | loop of Henlé | Bowman's capsule | collecting duct | glomerulus | second convoluted tubule

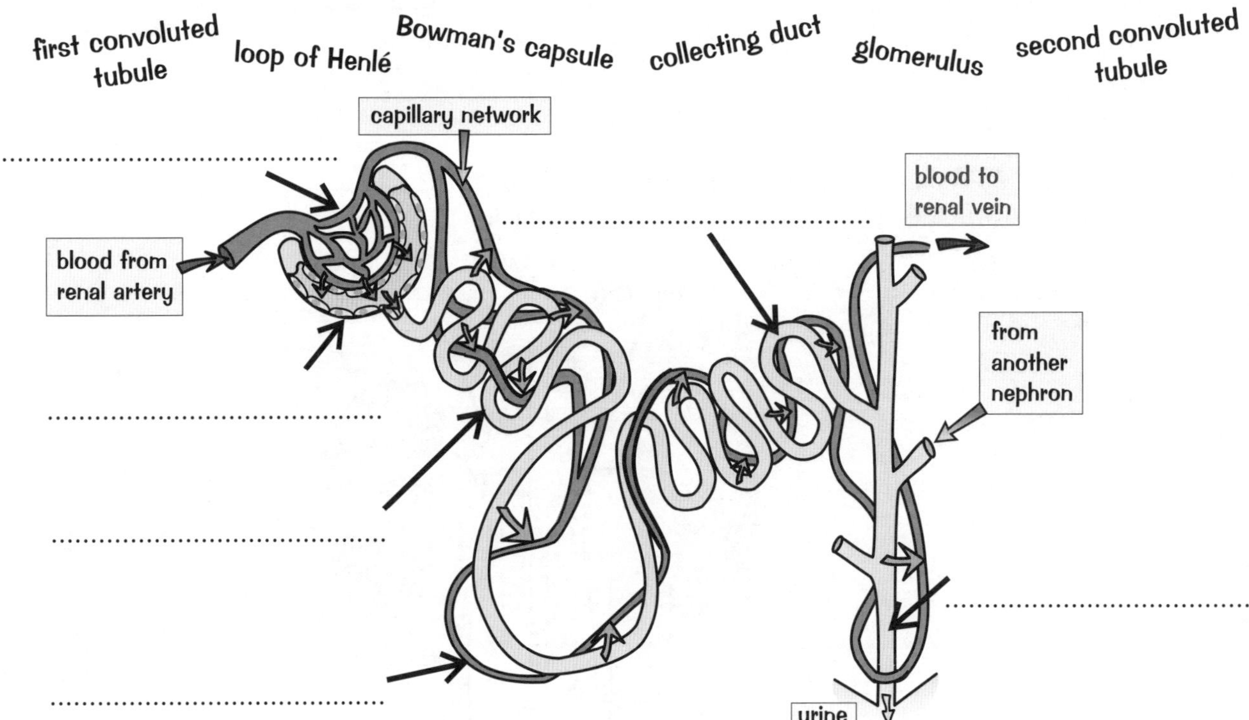

b) Draw a box on the diagram around the area where **filtration** happens.

Q5 The kidneys **control** the amount of **water** and other substances in the blood.

a) Name **one** substance that is **selectively reabsorbed** into the blood by the kidneys.

....

b) The kidneys maintain the right **water content** in the body. Give the name of this process.

....

c) What is excess water removed from the body in? ....

More on The Kidneys

Q1 The concentration of water in the blood is adjusted by the **kidneys**. They ensure that the water content never gets **too high** or **too low**.

a) What is the name given to the **homeostatic mechanism** by which water content is regulated?

....

b) Complete the diagram below by circling the correct word in each pair.

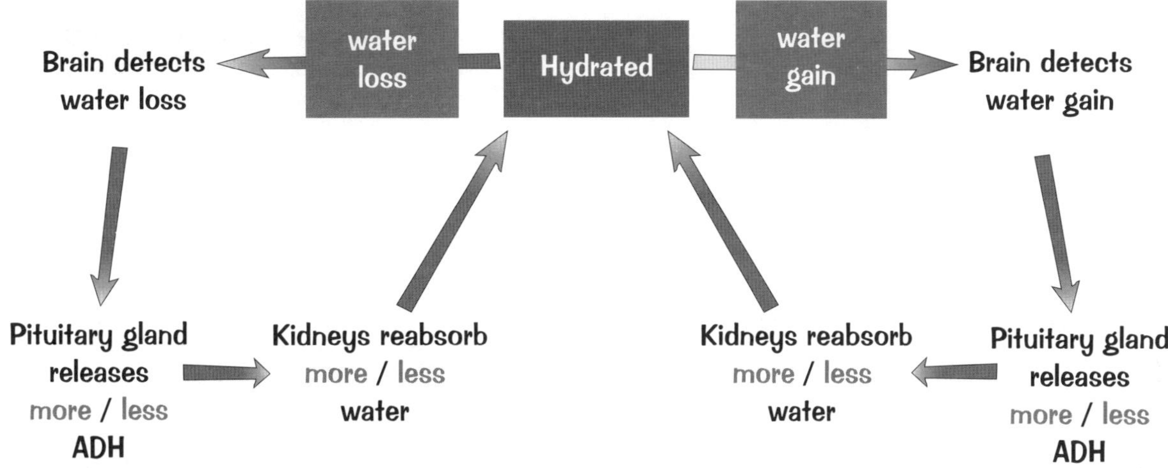

Q2 The graph shows the numbers of kidney transplant patients and numbers of donors in the **UK**.

a) **i)** Describe the trend in the number of people on the transplant waiting list.

....

....

....

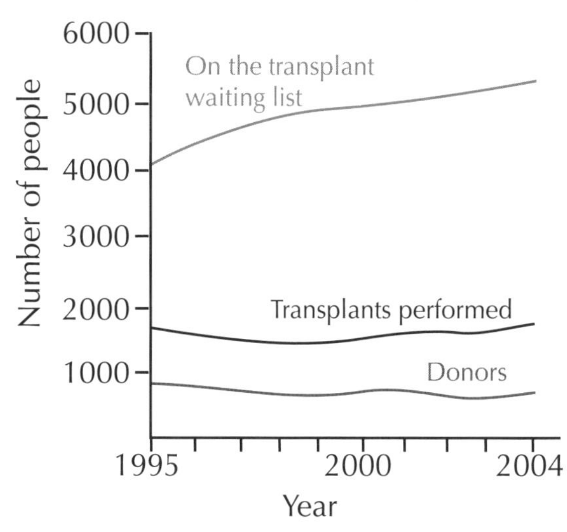

ii) What is the general trend for donors and transplants performed compared to the number of people on the transplant waiting list?

....

....

....

b) A donor kidney can be **rejected** by a patient's immune system. Suggest **one** precaution that could be taken to prevent this happening.

....

More on The Kidneys

Q3 If someone's kidneys fail they may be given a **kidney transplant** or they may have to use a **dialysis machine**. A dialysis machine does the job of the kidneys and filters the blood.

a) What substances would you expect a dialysis machine to **remove** from the blood? Tick the correct boxes.

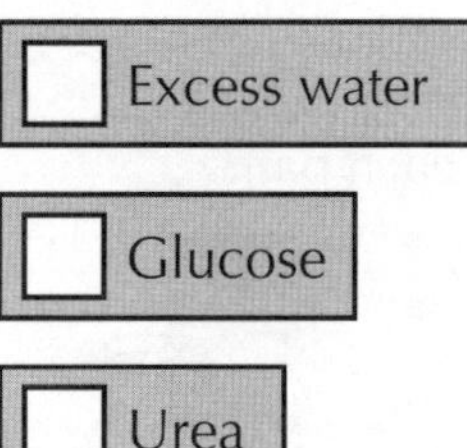

The new kidney opera house was less popular than the old one.

b) Add the correct labels to the dialysis diagram.

A Blood returned to patient

B Dialysis fluid in

C Selectively permeable barrier

D Dialysis fluid out

E Blood from patient

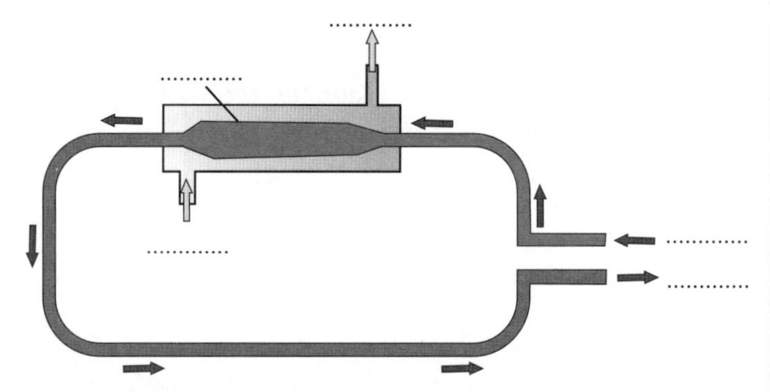

c) **i)** **How** does the composition of dialysis fluid compare with the composition of blood plasma?

....

ii) Why is this important?

....

d) The barrier is described as **selectively permeable**. What does this mean?

....

....

e) Explain why dialysis has to be carried out on a regular basis.

....

....

Top Tips: Dialysis is a clever technique that's saved lives. The problem is that it can take up to four hours to filter the blood and it has to be done a couple of times a week. An alternative is a kidney transplant — you can live with only one kidney, so it's possible for some people with kidney failure to receive a donated organ from a member of their family.

Reproductive Cells and The Menstrual Cycle

Q1 Below is a list of features of **reproductive cells**. Tick the boxes to show which ones are found in **sperm** and which ones are found in **eggs**.

		Sperm	Eggs
a)	a long tail	☐	☐
b)	enzymes to digest cell membranes	☐	☐
c)	nutrients in cell cytoplasm to feed the embryo	☐	☐
d)	lots of mitochondria	☐	☐

Q2 The diagram below shows how the **uterus lining** changes during the **menstrual cycle**.

Day: 1 Day: Day: Day:

a) Fill in the missing numbers for each day. Day 1 has been done for you.

b) Fill in the remaining boxes using the labels below:

Uterus lining builds up **Uterus lining maintained** **Egg released (ovulation)** **Uterus lining breaks down (menstruation)**

Q3 Sperm and eggs have **special features** to help them carry out their functions.

a) Fill in the blanks in the passage below by choosing some of the words from the box.

head energy egg sperm oxygen body middle acrosome

A .... cell has a long tail so that it can swim to the egg. It has lots of mitochondria in its .... section to provide the .... (from respiration) needed to swim a long way. It also has an .... at the front of its 'head'. This contains the enzymes needed to digest through the membrane of an .... cell.

b) After an egg is fertilised, the structure of its cell membrane changes. Explain why this happens.

....

c) Sperm and eggs have **haploid nuclei**.

i) What is a haploid nucleus? ....

ii) Explain why both sperm and eggs have haploid nuclei.

....

Menstrual Hormones

Q1 The menstrual cycle is controlled by four hormones: **FSH**, **LH**, **progesterone** and **oestrogen**. Complete the table below to show the effects of these by placing ticks in the correct boxes.

Effect	FSH	LH	Progesterone	Oestrogen
Stimulates oestrogen production				
Inhibits FSH production				
Causes uterus lining to thicken				
Causes a follicle to mature in an ovary				
Stimulates LH surge				
Stimulates ovulation				
Maintains uterus lining				

Q2 Circle the correct word(s) from each pair to complete the paragraph below.

During the menstrual cycle, hormone levels are controlled by negative **feedback** / **feedforward**. For example, FSH stimulates the ovary to release **oestrogen** / **progesterone**. This hormone then starts to **stimulate** / **inhibit** the release of FSH from the pituitary gland. After FSH has caused a follicle to mature, negative **feedback** / **feedforward** keeps FSH levels **high** / **low** so that **no more** / **lots more** follicles mature.

Q3 If a woman becomes pregnant, her levels of **progesterone** stay high.

a) Name the structure that secretes progesterone.

....

b) Explain why a woman's level of progesterone remains high throughout pregnancy. How does this help the developing baby?

....

....

....

c) Other than progesterone, the level of which hormone needs to drop for menstruation to occur?

....

Top Tips: Sometimes, it's haaard to be... a womaaan... Or a man for that matter, if you're trying to learn about menstrual hormones. This isn't really a topic where your natural intelligence and deep understanding of science can shine through much — you've just got to get your head down and learn what each hormone does. Sorry.

Fertility Treatments

Q1 Hormones can be used to **increase fertility**.

a) Underline **two** hormones from the list below that can be taken by a woman to increase her fertility.

FSH oestrogen insulin LH progesterone

b) Briefly explain how these hormones increase fertility.

....

c) Give **one** disadvantage of using hormones to increase fertility.

....

Q2 **Egg donation** can help a woman who can't produce eggs herself to have a child.

a) Other than being able to have a child, suggest **one** reason why a woman might choose to use donated eggs.

....

....

b) Suggest **one** disadvantage of using donated eggs to have a child.

....

Q3 ***In vitro*** **fertilisation** (**IVF**) can help couples to have children.

a) Explain how **IVF** works.

....

....

....

b) Discuss the advantages and disadvantages of IVF.

....

....

....

c) IVF can sometimes involve a **surrogate mother.**
What is a surrogate mother and when might one be used?

....

....

X and Y Chromosomes

Q1 Tick the boxes to show whether each statement is **true** or **false**.

		True	False
a)	Women have two X chromosomes. Men have an X and a Y chromosome.	☐	☐
b)	There is a 75% chance that a couple's first child will be a girl.	☐	☐
c)	Sperm cells (male gametes) can carry an X or a Y chromosome.	☐	☐
d)	If you have 4 children, you will always get 2 boys and 2 girls.	☐	☐

Q2 Here is a genetic diagram showing the inheritance of **sex chromosomes** in humans.

a) Complete the diagram to show the combinations of chromosomes in the offspring.

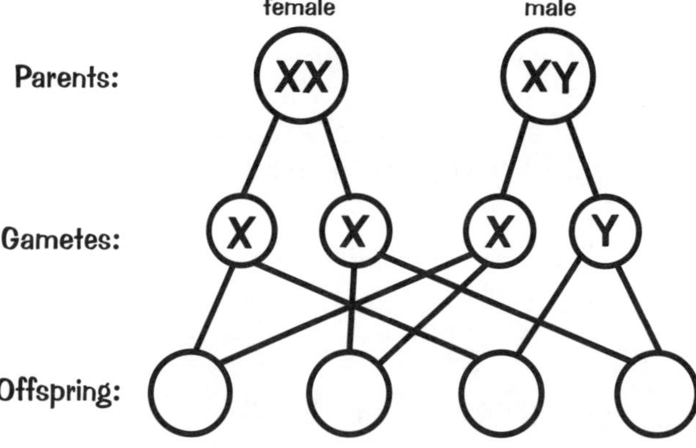

b) A woman becomes pregnant. What is the probability that the embryo is **male**?

....

Q3 **Birds** have sex chromosomes called **Z** and **W** (just like humans have X and Y). In birds, those with **two Z chromosomes** are **male**.

a) What are the female bird's sex chromosomes?

....

b) Complete the genetic diagram below to show the possible combination of gametes in bird reproduction.

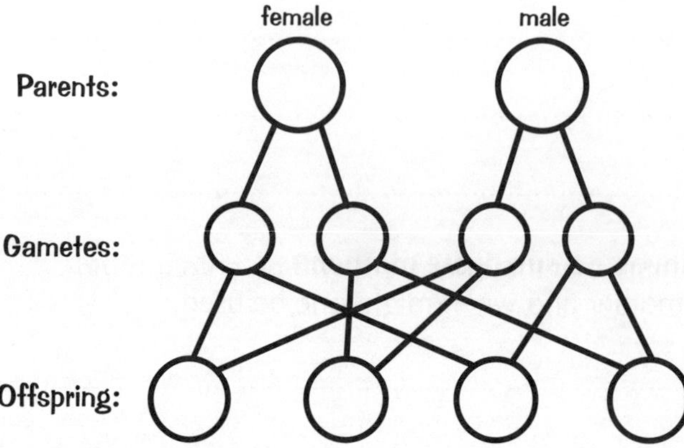

Sex-linked Genetic Disorders

Q1 **Haemophilia** is a sex-linked genetic disorder caused by a **faulty** blood clotting **allele**.

a) Explain what it means for a characteristic to be **sex-linked**.

....

b) The faulty allele is **recessive**. How many copies of the allele would the following people have:

i) a carrier .... **ii)** a sufferer ....

c) Complete the genetic diagram below to show the possible combinations of gametes from a **carrier** female and a **normal** (non-haemophiliac) male.

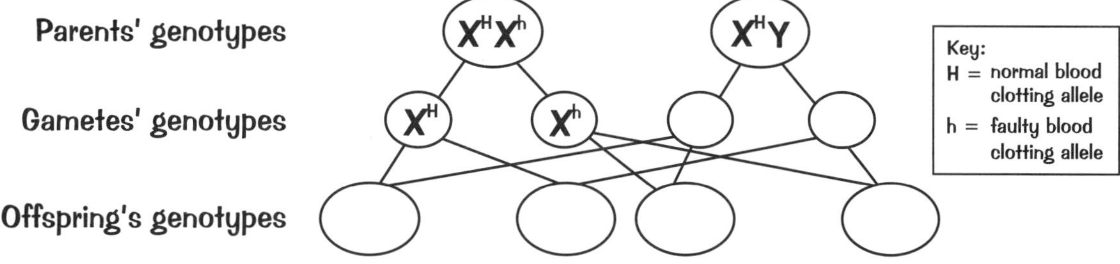

d) Find the probability of their offspring having haemophilia. ....

Q2 Joe is **colour blind**. His wife Becky is a **carrier** of the faulty colour vision allele.

a) Colour blindness is a sex-linked genetic disorder. Becky draws the diagram below to show Joe all the possible combinations of alleles that their children could inherit.

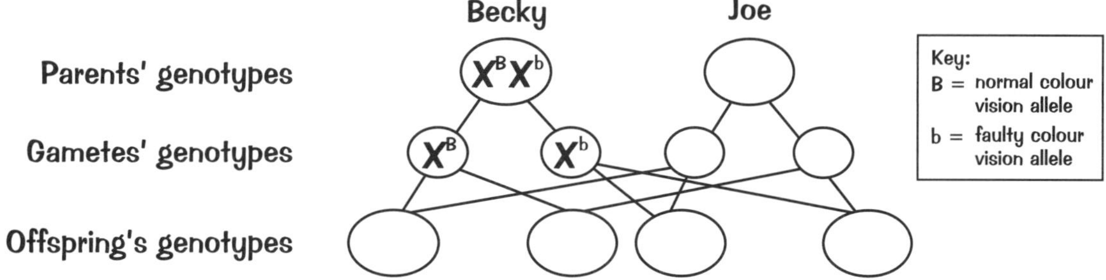

i) What is Joe's **genotype**? ....

ii) Fill in all the empty circles to complete Becky's diagram above.

b) Joe and Becky are expecting a baby.

i) What is the probability that their baby will be colour blind? ....

ii) Joe and Becky find out they're having a baby **girl**.
What is the probability that their baby girl will be colour blind? ....

Top Tips: Genetic crosses can be a bit of a faff to fill in — so take your time and work through the steps logically. After all that, you'll probably be asked to find the probability of something. Sorry.

Growth of Bacteria

Q1 Emily has a cut on her finger. **Bacteria** have got into the cut. The bacteria reproduce by **splitting into two** at regular intervals.

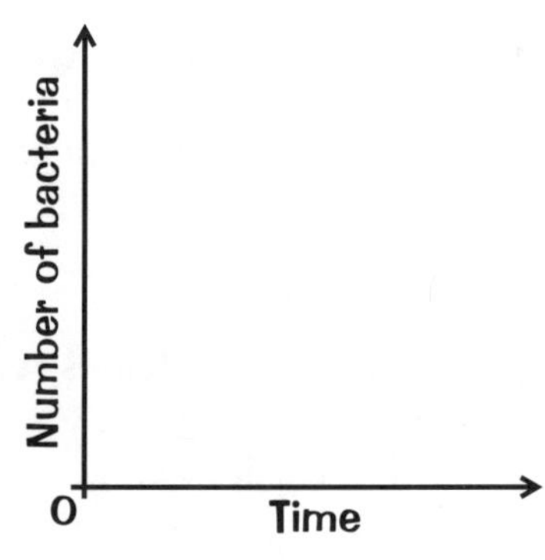

a) Use the axes on the right to sketch a graph showing how the population of bacteria will change over time.

b) Explain why the bacteria's ability to reproduce rapidly might be a problem for Emily.

....

....

Q2 **Pasteurisation** is a process used to kill off harmful microorganisms.

a) Fill in the blanks in the passage below.

> Pasteurisation involves .... a substance, then cooling it down. This kills off most harmful microbes, so the product shouldn't make you .... Any process like this which reduces contamination by germs is called an .... technique.

Bacteria resented being put out to pasture.

b) Name the person who invented pasteurisation. ....

Q3 Dan is investigating how **temperature** affects the **growth of bacteria**. He puts **milk** into three test tubes and adds **resazurin** dye. He stores each tube at either 5 °C, 15 °C or 30 °C for 24 hours.

a) Circle the colour of resazurin dye when there's plenty of oxygen around.

mauve blue colourless lilac pink

b) Suggest **one** thing that Dan should do to make his experiment a fair test.

....

c) The table on the right shows Dan's results after 0, 12 and 24 hours.

Time (hours)	0	12	24
Tube 1	Blue	Mauve	Colourless
Tube 2	Blue	Lilac	Mauve
Tube 3	Blue	Blue	Blue

i) Suggest which test tube Dan stored at 30 °C.

....

ii) Explain your answer to part **i)**.

Remember, bacteria grow faster at higher temperatures.

....

....

....

The Immune System

Q1 Underline the correct description of an **antigen**.

A chemical that causes disease.

A molecule found on the surface of a microorganism.

A 'foreign' cell.

A molecule that destroys bacteria.

Q2 Myra catches **mumps**, and then she recovers. Later on she is exposed to mumps again. The graph below shows how the level of the **antibody against mumps** in Myra's blood **changes** over time.

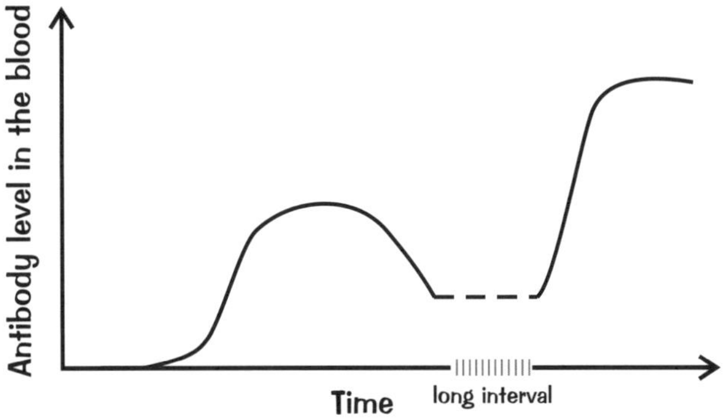

Antibody level in the blood

Time

long interval

a) Write an '**X**' on the graph at the point where Myra was exposed to the mumps virus for the **first** time.

b) Write a '**Y**' on the graph at the point where Myra was exposed to the mumps virus for the **second** time.

c) After the first infection, Myra's body produces a special type of cell that helps her respond to the virus **faster** the second time around. Give the name of this type of cell.

....

Q3 John catches **chickenpox**. For about a week he has an itchy rash all over his skin, with a headache and a slight fever. Then the rash begins to clear up and John starts to feel better.

a) Describe how John's immune system gets rid of the chickenpox virus.

....

....

....

b) Five years later, John and his friend Jim are exposed to chickenpox at university. Jim has never had chickenpox before. Explain why Jim becomes ill, but John doesn't.

....

....

....

....

Immunisation

Q1 **Edward Jenner** invented the first vaccine, against smallpox. He came up with the idea after noticing that people who had cowpox didn't catch smallpox.

The sentences below describe the experiment that Jenner performed to test his idea. Number the sentences to show their correct order.

The first one has been done for you.

- [ ] **The boy was a bit unwell, but then recovered.**
- [1] **Jenner took some bits of scab from a girl with cowpox.**
- [ ] **Jenner exposed the boy to smallpox.**
- [ ] **Jenner placed the bits of scab into a cut on the arm of a boy.**
- [ ] **The boy didn't catch smallpox.**

Q2 **Immunisation** involves injecting dead or inactive microorganisms into the body.

a) Why do dead microorganisms cause the body to produce antibodies?

....

....

b) Tick the boxes to show whether the statements below about polio immunisation are **true** or **false**.

	True	False
i) The dead or inactive polio microorganisms have some of the same antigens as the live pathogen.	☐	☐
ii) B-lymphocytes produce antibodies against the antigens on the injected polio microorganisms.	☐	☐
iii) The antigens on the dead or inactive polio microorganisms don't trigger memory lymphocytes to be made.	☐	☐

Q3 a) Give two **benefits** of immunisation.

1. ....

2. ....

b) Give two **risks** of immunisation.

1. ....

2. ....

Monoclonal Antibodies

Q1 The diagram on the right shows how **monoclonal antibodies** are produced in the lab.

a) Fill in the missing labels on the diagram using the words below.

tumour cells | hybridoma | antigen | monoclonal antibodies

b) Explain why monoclonal antibodies aren't made directly from either B-lymphocytes or tumour cells.

....

....

....

....

....

Q2 Monoclonal antibodies are used in **pregnancy test sticks**. They detect a **hormone** that's found in the urine of women **only** when they are pregnant.

a) Draw lines to match the beginning of each sentence to the correct ending.

The bit of the stick you wee on...	...has antibodies to the hormone stuck to it (so they can't move).
The test strip...	...has antibodies to the hormone, with blue beads attached.

b) The statements below describe what happens if you **are pregnant** and you wee on the testing stick. Number them to show their correct order. The first one has been done for you.

- [1] The hormone binds to the antibodies on the blue beads.
- [ ] The beads and hormone bind to the antibodies on the test strip
- [ ] The blue beads get stuck on the test strip, turning it blue.
- [ ] The urine moves up the stick, carrying the hormone and the beads.

The test strip goes blue if you're pregnant.

c) Explain why the test strip **doesn't** turn blue if someone who is **not pregnant** wees on the stick.

....

....

Top Tips: Before some clever bods came up with the method shown above, it was really hard to make antibodies in the lab. Now they're used for all sorts of things — even sticks that you wee on...

More on Monoclonal Antibodies

Q1 Tick the boxes to show whether each statement is **true** or **false**.

		True	False
a)	Different cells in the body have identical antigens on their cell surface.	☐	☐
b)	You can make monoclonal antibodies that will bind to specific cells in the body.	☐	☐
c)	Cancer cells don't have any antigens on their cell membranes.	☐	☐

Q2 Monoclonal antibodies can be used to **diagnose cancer**.

a) Circle the correct word from each pair to complete the passage below.

> Antibodies that will bind to **body cells / tumour markers** are labelled with a radioactive element. The labelled antibodies are given to a patient through a drip. When the antibodies come into contact with the **body / cancer** cells, they bind to the tumour markers. A picture of the patient's body is taken using a camera that detects **radioactivity / movement**. Anywhere there are cancer cells will show up as a **dark / bright** spot.

b) Give **two** things that a doctor can tell by looking at a picture of labelled cancer cells.

....

c) Name **one** other medical problem that monoclonal antibodies can be used to diagnose.

....

Q3 Monoclonal antibodies can also be used to **treat cancer**.

a) The diagrams below show the correct order of steps in this process.
Draw lines to match each label to its correct diagram.

1 + →

2

3 normal body cells cancer cell

4

The antibodies bind to the tumour markers on the cancer cells.	An anti-cancer drug is attached to monoclonal antibodies.	The drug kills the cancer cells but doesn't kill any normal body cells near the tumour.	The antibodies are given to the patient through a drip.

b) Explain why it might be better for a patient to be treated with an antibody-labelled drug rather than other cancer treatments.

....

....

Drugs From Plants and Plant Diseases

Q1 Many new **drugs** that are developed are based on chemicals produced by **plants**.

a) Fill in the blanks in the passage below using the words from the box.

pathogens   symptoms   traditional   defend   drugs

Plants produce chemicals to .... themselves against pests and .... Some of these chemicals can be used as .... to treat human diseases or relieve .... A lot of our current medicines were discovered by studying plants used in .... cures.

b) i) Name a medical drug that humans have developed from plants. ....

ii) What condition or symptoms is the drug you have named in part **i)** used to treat?

....

Q2 Brussel Farm grows a vegetable called **sprotilicious**. The farmers record the **crop yield** in their fields each week. The data for March is given in the table below.

Date	Sprotilicious Crop Yield (tonnes)
1st March	60
8th March	51
15th March	36
22nd March	6
29th March	0

a) Draw a **bar chart** showing the change in tonnes of sprotilicious during March on the grid above.

b) i) Describe the trend shown by the graph.

....

ii) Suggest what might have caused the trend shown in the graph.

....

iii) What impact might the trend shown by the graph have on consumers?

....

Daily Rhythms

Q1 Sleep patterns are an example of a **circadian rhythm**.

a) What is a circadian rhythm?

....

b) Are circadian rhythms controlled **internally** or **externally**?

....

c) Other than sleep patterns, give **one** example of a circadian rhythm.

....

Q2 Plants show lots of different **photoperiodic responses**.

a) Tick the box next to the correct definition of a 'photoperiodic response'.

- A response to a change in the amount of light and dark in a 12 hour cycle. ☐
- A response to a change in the amount of light and dark in a 24 hour cycle. ☐
- Plant growth towards light. ☐
- Plant growth towards gravity. ☐

online @ PlantBook

Daisy's Photos

b) Explain why some plants:

i) only germinate when the days are very long.

....

....

ii) only flower when the day is at least a certain length.

....

....

iii) only grow when the day length is increasing.

....

....

Top Tips: Plants might look all sweet and innocent and dull, but don't let them fool you. They've got sneaky little ways of making sure they do the right stuff at the right time of the year. They're as crafty as a teacher plotting an exam revision timetable...

Mixed Questions — B3 Topic 1

Q1 **Fertilisation** happens when a **sperm cell** fuses with an **egg cell**.
The resulting embryo grows and develops during pregnancy.

a) **i)** What is the probability that the embryo formed will be male? ....

ii) Circle the genotype the embryo will have if it is male. **XX** **XY**

b) Name the hormone that maintains the uterus lining during pregnancy. ....

c) Circle the correct word(s) from each pair to complete the paragraph below.

> Pregnancy test sticks detect a hormone found in a woman's urine only when she **is / isn't** pregnant. The test strip has **antigens / antibodies** stuck to it that can bind to this hormone. The bit you wee on contains blue beads with the same **antigens / antibodies** attached. If a woman's pregnant, the hormone binds to the **antigens / antibodies** on the blue beads. The **urine / antigen** moves up the stick, carrying the hormone and the beads. The beads and hormone bind to the antibodies on the test strip, turning it **blue / colourless**.

Q2

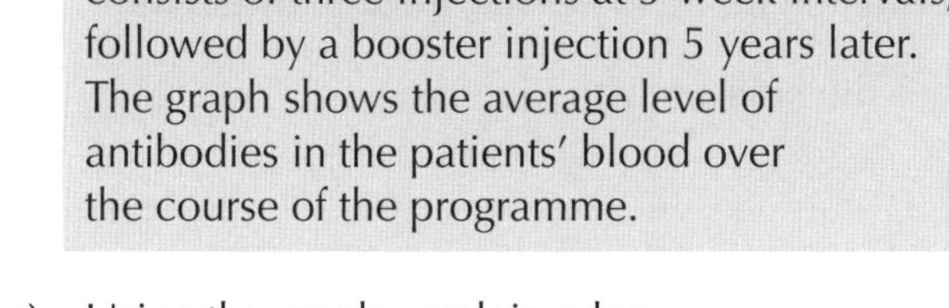

A **course of immunisation** against **disease B** consists of three injections at 5-week intervals, followed by a booster injection 5 years later. The graph shows the average level of antibodies in the patients' blood over the course of the programme.

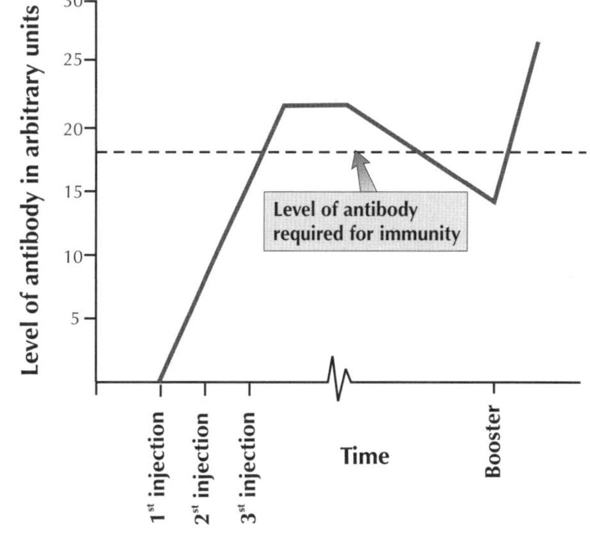

a) Using the graph, explain why:

i) Three injections are needed initially.

....

....

ii) A booster injection is needed after 5 years.

....

b) Explain how **immunisation** works.

....

....

....

Mixed Questions — B3 Topic 1

Q3 The diagram represents the **menstrual cycle** in a particular woman. At day 14 the woman **ovulates**.

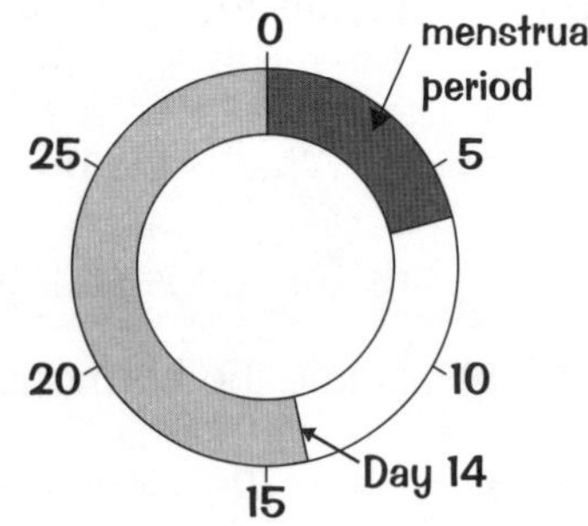

a) Which hormone triggers ovulation? ....

b) **Oestrogen** is one of the four main hormones that control the menstrual cycle. Give **two** functions of oestrogen.

1. ....

2. ....

c) Another key hormone in the menstrual cycle is **FSH**. A woman with **low** levels of FSH may **not** be able to get pregnant.

i) Why is it unlikely that a woman with low levels of FSH will be able to get pregnant?

....

ii) This type of infertility can usually be treated with injections of FSH. Give **two** other ways that infertility can be treated.

1. ....

2. ....

Q4 The **kidneys** perform the vital function of **filtering** the blood to get rid of **waste products**.

a) Give the name of the blood vessel that supplies the kidneys with blood.

....

b) The table shows the number of UK patients with **kidney failure** in **2004** and predicted numbers for **2013**.

i) Calculate the number of patients who received a **kidney transplant** in **2004**. Write your answer in the table.

Assume that the patients with kidney failure will either be receiving dialysis or will have received a transplant.

	Year	
	2004	**2013**
Total number of patients with kidney failure	37 000	68 000
Number receiving dialysis	20 500	
Number that have received a transplant		30 000

ii) Calculate the number of patients who are likely to be receiving **dialysis** in **2013**. Write your answer in the table.

c) This table shows the cost of each treatment.

Treatment	Average cost per patient (£)
Dialysis	30 000 per year
Transplant	20 000
Anti-rejection drugs	6 500 per year

Calculate the amount of money saved per patient when a **transplant** is performed instead of **three** years of **dialysis**.

....

....

Don't forget that transplant patients need drugs to stop organ rejection.

Innate and Learned Behaviour

Q1 Read the following passage and fill in the missing words, using some of the words below.

genes   environment   learned   responsive   innate

Behaviour in animals can be inherited or ....
— or a combination of the two. Inherited behaviour is known as .... behaviour. Inherited aspects of behaviour depend on the animal's ....

Q2 Draw lines to match up the aspects of **human behaviour** to show whether they are **innate** or **learned**.

Playing football   innate   Salivating

Sneezing   learned   Language

Q3 **Habituation** is an important part of the learning process in young animals.

a) Explain the term **habituation**.

....

....

b) Explain why habituation is **beneficial** to animals.

....

Q4 **Imprinting** is a type of behaviour seen in some animals.

a) What is **imprinting**?

....

....

b) Is imprinting a **learned behaviour**, an **innate behaviour**, or a **combination** of the two?

....

c) Name **one** type of animal that shows imprinting behaviour.

....

Innate and Learned Behaviour

Q5 An experiment was carried out into the **feeding behaviour** of **sea anemones**. Sea anemones are simple animals that live in marine rock pools, where they are found attached to rocks. Each has a ring of **tentacles** armed with stinging cells. Anemones use the stinging cells to paralyse smaller animals swimming in the water.

Two tanks of sea water each contained a single sea anemone. The behaviour of both the sea anemones was observed for **one hour**. A volume of 'fish extract' (made by crushing some dead fish in sea water) was placed in **one** of the tanks at a certain point within the hour of observation. The number of moving tentacles for each sea anemone was recorded at five minute intervals.

Time / minutes	No. of moving tentacles	
	Tank A	Tank B
0	2	2
5	1	1
10	10	2
15	7	0
20	4	2
30	3	0
40	4	0
50	4	1
60	4	2

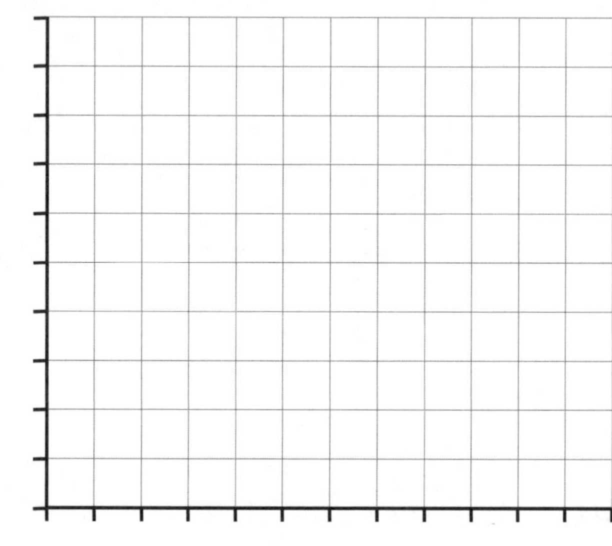

Time / minutes

a) Draw graphs to illustrate the data on the grid provided. Use the same axes to show the results for both tanks.

b) Do you think the fish extract was added to **tank A** or to **tank B**? Explain your answer.

....

....

c) Suggest a time when the extract was added to the tank, giving a reason for your answer.

....

d) Suggest an explanation for what happened in the tank to which extract was added.

....

....

e) Do you think that this response is an example of **learned** or **innate** behaviour?

....

Top Tips: Animals are born with all the **nerve pathways** they need for **innate** behaviours **already connected**. The nerve pathways needed for **learned** behaviours develop with experience.

Conditioning

Q1 **Conditioning** is a type of **learned behaviour**.

a) Explain the difference between '**classical** conditioning' and '**operant** conditioning'.

....

....

....

....

b) Identify each of the following examples of behaviour as either **classical conditioning** (**C**) or **operant conditioning** (**O**).

	C	O
i) A baby receives food, which makes it naturally happy. It only gets food when its mother is present. When its mother is present it feels happiness.	☐	☐
ii) A rat is provided with a maze, at the end of which is a food reward. After many trials, the rat learns to complete the maze and reach the reward without error.	☐	☐
iii) A child learns how to ride a bike.	☐	☐
iv) A dolphin learns to associate being given food with its trainer blowing a whistle.	☐	☐

Q2 **Police sniffer dogs** undergo a period of intensive training. This involves teaching the dogs to **find illegal substances**, like drugs, and **alert their handlers** to what they've found.

a) Suggest **one** form of **operant conditioning** that could be used to encourage a dog to find an illegal substance and then alert their handler.

....

b) Give **one** other example of operant conditioning being used to train animals in the police force.

....

Q3 Describe **one** example of when classical conditioning is used **in combination** with operant conditioning when training captive animals.

....

....

....

....

Social Behaviour and Communication

Q1 List three reasons why animals **communicate** with one another.

1. ....

2. ....

3. ....

Q2 Below is a list of different **types** of communication used by different kinds of animals. In each case, suggest a **reason** for the communication.

a) A peacock raises and shakes its long coloured tail feathers.

....

b) A butterfly flashes its wings to show spots that look like large, staring eyes.

....

c) A honey bee does a 'waggle dance' in the hive.

....

d) A dog rolls onto its back.

....

Q3 Some animals use **pheromones** to communicate.

a) What is a pheromone?

....

b) Suggest why a female moth might release a pheromone into the air.

....

Q4 The **chiffchaff** and the **willow warbler** are two related species of woodland birds. They are both green-brown in colour and spend much of their time among the foliage of trees.

Suggest why these birds attract mates using song rather than visual signals.

....

Animal Behaviour Studies

Q1 Draw lines to match the ethologist to their research.

Jane Goodall	Imprinting in geese.
Nikolaas Tinbergen	Social behaviour in gorillas.
Dian Fossey	Social behaviour in chimpanzees.
Konrad Lorenz	Innate behaviour in gulls.

Q2 Describe how **imprinting** is a beneficial behaviour for goose chicks.

....

Q3 Give **two** examples of social behaviour in gorillas and chimpanzees.

1. ....

2. ....

Q4 Experiments were carried out to investigate feeding behaviour in young **herring gulls**. The young peck at the bill of the parent to stimulate it to regurgitate fish, which the young then swallow. This behaviour occurs soon after the young hatch. Scientists presented young herring gulls with a series of **cardboard models** of a parent gull's head. The results of the study are shown below. Real adult herring gulls have a **white head**, with a **yellow bill** and a **red spot** near the tip.

Model	White head, grey bill, no spot	White head, grey bill, red spot	White head, yellow bill, red spot	Pointed red stick with three white bands
No. of pecks by young	5	39	42	50

a) Describe what these experiments demonstrate about what stimulates feeding behaviour in young herring gulls. Explain your answer.

....

....

....

b) Is this behaviour innate or learned? Give a reason for your answer.

....

Investigating Animal Behaviour

Q1 Tick the correct box to show whether each of the statements below is **true** or **false**.

		True	False
a)	A choice chamber is a container with one big chamber in the middle.	☐	☐
b)	Choice chambers are often used to investigate the behaviour of insects.	☐	☐
c)	In a choice chamber, an animal will usually head to environmental conditions that are closest to their natural habitat.	☐	☐
d)	You can use choice chambers to investigate how animals respond to genetic factors.	☐	☐
e)	Once an animal goes into one of the chambers they can't get out again.	☐	☐

Q2 Jerry wanted to investigate woodlice behaviour. He set up a **choice chamber** with four different sections, as shown on the right. He put **10 woodlice** into the centre and then put the lid on. After 15 minutes, he recorded the number of woodlice in each chamber. His results are shown in the table.

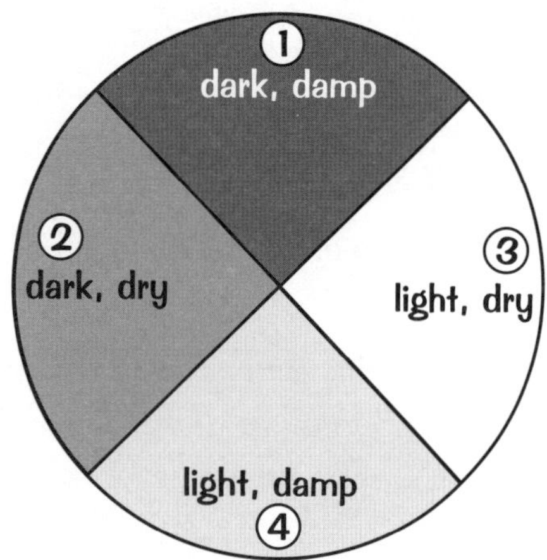

Chamber	1	2	3	4
No. of woodlice	7	2	1	0

a) Suggest why Jerry put all the woodlice into the centre of the choice chamber at the beginning of the experiment.

....

b) **i)** Describe what the results show about the conditions woodlice prefer.

....

....

....

ii) Suggest why the woodlice prefer these conditions in the choice chamber.

....

....

c) Give **two** conditions that Jerry should have controlled in his experiment to make it a fair test.

1. ....

2. ....

Mating Behaviour

Q1 Different **species** can have very different **mating strategies**.

Circle the correct word from each pair to complete these sentences about mating behaviour.

a) **Monogamy** / **Courtship** means staying with just one mate for life.
It's pretty **common** / **rare** in the animal kingdom.

b) In many species one **male** / **female** will mate with several **males** / **females** during one breeding season.

c) In some mammals, one male has a group of females and mates with **all** / **none** of them, e.g. **gibbons** / **lions**.

Q2 **Swans** mate for life — once a pair have mated, they only breed with each other.
Explain why this behaviour is unusual, and describe some more common mating patterns.

....

....

....

Q3 **Male frigate birds** have red sacs on their chests. During the mating season, males **display** by inflating this sac, as shown in the picture.

a) What type of behaviour is this?

....

b) What advantage might the male frigate bird gain from this behaviour?

....

....

c) In most bird species the female is **duller** in appearance than the male. Explain why this is.

....

....

....

Mating Behaviour

Q4 In most species, **males compete** to win the right to mate with females. Methods used vary from bringing the female gifts of food to fighting off the other males. However, it is the **opposite** way around in **seahorses** — females compete for the attention of males. Seahorses are also unusual in that the female lays her eggs in the male's pouch and **he** is then '**pregnant**' with the young and eventually gives birth to them.

a) Explain fully why males usually compete for females, and suggest why this is not the case in seahorses.

....

....

....

....

....

b) Why is it important for most animals that females don't mate with a male of a closely related species?

....

....

Q5 Male **crickets** and **grasshoppers** attract females by a process called '**stridulation**', where they rub rough parts of their body together. Crickets rub their wings together and grasshoppers rub their legs over their wings. The result is a **chirping sound**.

a) Different species of crickets and grasshoppers produce different patterns of chirps, in terms of volume, pitch and frequency of chirps. Suggest why.

....

b) The 'songs' of different species of grasshopper are more distinctive than the songs of different species of cricket. What does this suggest about the **appearance** of different species of the two kinds of insects. Explain your answer.

....

....

....

Top Tips: The male **bowerbird** impresses females by constructing an elaborate mound of earth decorated lavishly with shells, leaves, feathers and flowers, which he spends **hours** carefully arranging.

Parenting Behaviour

Q1 In many species of **birds**, **both** parents play a role in incubating eggs and feeding the young once the eggs have hatched.

a) State an advantage of this shared responsibility for:

i) the young. ....

....

ii) the parents. ....

....

b) **Birds of paradise** differ in that the females have sole responsibility for looking after the young. These birds live on the island of New Guinea, where there are few predators.

Suggest a possible link between the reproductive behaviour of birds of paradise and the fact that there are few predators in their habitat.

....

....

....

Q2 Some animals **care for their young** for long periods, while others provide **no parental care** at all.

a) Give **three** ways in which animals may care for their young.

1. ....

2. ....

3. ....

b) Explain how caring for their young may put the parents at **risk**.

Think about how doing the things you listed in part a) might cause problems for the parents.

....

....

....

Q3 Explain why parental care can be a **successful evolutionary strategy**.

....

....

Parenting Behaviour

Q4 The table compares the **average number of offspring** produced per female per year for some different animal species.

Species	Average number of offspring per year
Orang-utan	0.25
Wood mouse	20
Sperm whale	0.1
Red fox	5
Green turtle	200

a) Explain how it is possible for the average number of offspring per year of the orang-utan and the sperm whale to be less than one.

....

....

b) On average, a female wood mouse gives birth to **five** offspring after a pregnancy. Explain how 20 offspring can be produced per year.

....

c) Which species of animal is likely to show the least degree of parental care? Give a full explanation for your answer.

....

....

....

....

d) Which species of animal is likely to have the greatest proportion of their young survive? Explain your answer.

....

....

....

Top Tips: Ah, parents — we'd be stuffed without them. We'd have no-one to make our tea, do our ironing or mop our sweaty brows when we were sick. But worst of all we'd have no-one's bank balance to drain. And all we have to do is put up with a bit of nagging. Seems fair to me.

Plant Communication and Co-evolution

Q1 Use the words provided to complete the paragraph below about how insects help to **pollinate** plants.

plants	nectar	pollen	chemicals

Lots of flowers are scented — they release smelly .... to attract insects. The insects come to the flower looking for sugary .... While they're there, some .... gets stuck to them. When they fly away, they carry it with them and pass it on to other ....

Eau de Sugar

Q2 When some plants are **eaten by insect pests** they release **chemicals**.

a) Some of these chemicals attract **insect predators**. Explain how these predators help the plant.

....

b) Plants can also communicate with **nearby plants** using the chemicals they release. Explain how this helps the nearby plants.

....

....

Q3 The **button-plant** produces chemicals in its nectar which kill insects that try to eat it. But Professor Route has discovered a species of **butterfly** that **can** eat the nectar. She thinks the button-plant and the butterfly might have **co-evolved**.

a) What is co-evolution?

....

b) Do you think the button-plant and the butterfly co-evolved? Explain your answer.

....

....

....

....

Mmm, tasty.

Fossil Evidence for Human Evolution

Q1 Draw lines to connect each fossil or group of fossils to the correct **age**.

Ardi	3.2 million years old
Lucy	1.6 million years old
Hominids discovered by Leaky	4.4 million years old

Q2 Circle the correct word in each pair to complete the sentences about **Ardi** below.

a) Ardi had **long** / **short** arms and **long** / **short** legs — more like an ape than a human.

b) She had an **ape-like** / **human-like** toe.

c) Her brain was about the same size as a **chimpanzee** / **human**.

d) The structure of Ardi's legs suggests she walked like a **chimpanzee** / **human**.

e) Her hand bones suggest that she **did** / **didn't** use her hands to help her walk.

Q3 Use the words provided to complete the paragraph below.

You can use each word once, more than once, or not at all.

smaller	human	short	larger	walking upright	climbing trees	ape	long

Turkana-boy, a fossil discovered by Leakey, is more like a ....
than Lucy. His .... arms and .... legs
are much more like a .... than an ....
His brain size was much .... than Lucy's. The structure of his
legs and feet suggests he was better adapted to ....

Q4 **Lucy** is a fossil hominid who was found in Ethiopia.

a) Is Lucy **more** or **less** human-like than the fossil Ardi?

....

b) Explain your answer to part **a)**.

....

....

....

More Evidence for Human Evolution

Q1 Studying **mitochondrial DNA** can help us to understand how humans have **evolved**.

a) Tick the correct boxes to show whether the statements below are **true** or **false**.

	True	False
i) You inherit all of your mitochondrial DNA from your father.	☐	☐
ii) Everyone on the planet has similar mitochondrial DNA.	☐	☐
iii) Studying mitochondrial DNA has shown that everyone is descended from one woman — 'Mitochondrial Eve'.	☐	☐

b) Choose words from the box to fill in the gaps in the passage below.

high evolved migrated 200 000 Africa mutations

Some bits of mitochondrial DNA vary from person to person due to ....

Mitochondrial DNA has a .... mutation rate. Scientists studying the changes in mitochondrial DNA have worked out that 'Mitochondrial Eve' lived in .... about .... years ago. This means that *Homo sapiens* must have .... there, and then .... to other areas of the world.

Mitochondrial Eve is also known as African Eve.

Q2 The **stone tools** shown on the right are part of a museum display about **human evolution**.

Tool A

Tool B

a) **i)** Circle the tool that you think was made **most recently**.

ii) Explain your answer to part **i)**.

....

....

....

b) The label in the museum next to Tool B says that it is approximately 200 000 years old. Describe **one** way that scientists might have worked out how old it is.

....

....

Q3 Both **mitochondrial DNA** and **nuclear DNA** can be used to study **human evolution**.

Give **two** reasons why mitochondrial DNA can be more useful for this than nuclear DNA.

1. ....

2. ....

Climate Change and Human Behaviour

Q1 Humans lived through the last **ice age**, which brought about a change in temperature and food that was available to eat. As their **environment changed**, humans **changed their behaviour** so that they could survive in the new environment.

a) What is an ice age?

....

....

b) Suggest how humans changed their behaviour to cope with:

i) the change in temperature.

....

....

ii) the change in food availability.

....

....

Q2 When humans **migrated** out of Africa they found lots of **new environments**. For example, in Europe they found a new range of plants, much larger animals, and that it was much colder.

a) Suggest how the behaviour of humans changed when they arrived in Europe.

....

....

....

b) **i)** Give another example of an area that humans migrated to from Africa.

....

ii) Give **one** change that occurred in their behaviour when humans migrated to the area you named in part **i)**.

Think about how the place you named would be **different** to what they were used to before.

....

....

Top Tips: The last **real** ice age ended more than 10 000 years ago — but we've had some cold blips since then. For example, things got a bit chilly between the 16th and 19th centuries — it was so cold in winter that the Thames used to freeze and people held a fair on the ice. Brrrr.

Mixed Questions — B3 Topic 2

Q1 Many people keep **dogs** either as **companions** or as **working** animals. The domesticated dog is similar in many ways to **wild dogs** which live in parts of Africa.

a) A domesticated dog can be taught to 'sit' by rewarding it every time it responds correctly to the 'sit' command. What type of conditioning is this an example of? Underline the correct answer.

classical **operant**

b) Many domesticated dogs are useful as guards, because they will bark loudly if they hear a burglar breaking into the house, but don't bark at noises from people or cars just passing the house.

Suggest why dogs respond to the quiet noise of a burglar but not to the louder noise from cars.

....

....

c) Dogs often communicate with other dogs using chemicals, for example to mark their territories. What are these chemicals called?

....

d) Both wild dogs and domesticated dogs feed their young on milk for several weeks after birth. How does a newborn puppy 'know' to suckle from its mother?

....

e) After birth, young wild dogs spend several months with their parents, who protect them from predators and teach them to hunt effectively.

i) Outline the possible **disadvantages** for the parents of this behaviour.

....

ii) Explain why this behaviour is a **good evolutionary strategy**, despite its disadvantages.

....

....

Q2 Most **birds** reproduce by laying a **small** clutch of eggs, and keeping them warm until they hatch into **chicks**. They then tend the chicks in the nest for several weeks.

a) **Frogs** lay **large** clumps of frogspawn in a pond and then leave — they don't tend the spawn or the tadpoles which hatch from it. Explain why frogs don't need to look after their young but birds do.

....

....

b) The 'cheeping' of a young bird stimulates its parent to feed it. Give two other 'uses' of bird calls.

....

Large-scale Growth of Microorganisms

Q1 Complete the passage about **biotechnology** by filling in the gaps using the words below.

dead	microorganisms	mammals	useful	services	living

Biotechnology means using .... organisms, especially ...., to produce .... products (e.g. food or medicines) or to provide people with .... (e.g. waste management or water purification).

Q2 The diagram on the right shows a **fermenter**.

a) What is a fermenter?

....

....

....

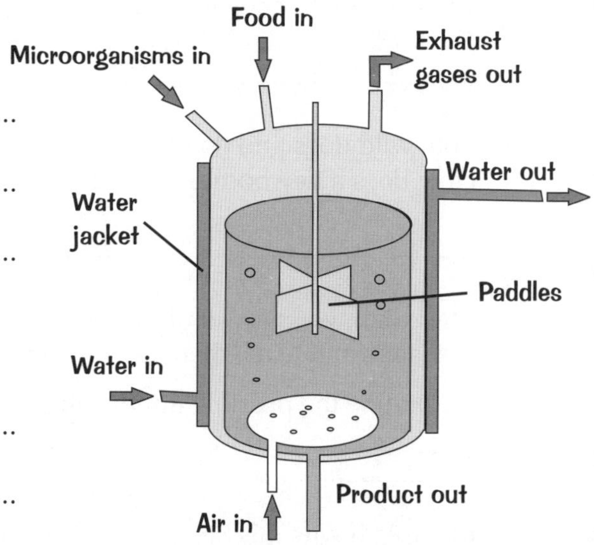

b) Why is it important for a fermenter to have the right conditions?

....

....

....

Think about the conditions microorganisms need to grow to help you answer part c).

c) Explain the purpose of each of the following:

i) the water jacket

....

ii) the air supply

....

iii) the paddles

....

d) Explain why aseptic conditions are needed in the fermenter.

....

Large-scale Growth of Microorganisms

Q3 The diagram on the right shows an experiment to investigate the effects of different factors on **yeast growth** under **anaerobic conditions**.

yeast suspension

lime water

a) Describe the changes you would expect to see in the lime water and explain why.

....

....

b) Suggest **one** way you could measure the yeast's **rate of respiration**.

....

....

c) Give **two** factors that are likely to affect the respiration rate of yeast.

1. ....

2. ....

Q4 A group of students set up the experiment below to simulate the conditions in a **fermenter**.

1. **Make up the culture medium and put it into a sterile flask.**
2. **Add a sample of the microorganism (yeast).**
3. **Seal the flask with a ventilated bung that lets gas out but not in.**
4. **Mix thoroughly then place in the incubator at 37 °C.**
5. **Remove from the incubator for mixing every 15 minutes.**

a) George set up his experiment but forgot to put the flask into the incubator. Suggest what effect this would have on his experiment.

....

b) The teacher asked pupils to take a small sample of their culture medium and test it with Universal Indicator paper. Why did they need to do this?

....

c) Do you think that the yeast cells were respiring aerobically or anaerobically? Explain your answer.

....

Microorganisms and Food

Q1 Complete the passage about **yoghurt making** by filling in the gaps using the words below.

fermenter cooled lactose ferment clot
pasteurised lactic acid bacteria incubated

To make yoghurt, milk is .... to kill off any unwanted microorganisms, then .... Next, a starter culture of .... is added and the mixture is .... in a ....
The bacteria .... the .... sugar in the milk to form .... This causes the milk to .... and form yoghurt.

Q2 **Mycoprotein** is a food source that comes from fungi.

a) What is mycoprotein used to replace in food?

....

b) Give **one** advantage of using mycoprotein as a food source.

....

c) Name the fungus that mycoprotein is made from.

....

Q3 Give three advantages of producing **foods** using **microorganisms** rather than other organisms.

1. ....

2. ....

3. ....

Q4 Yoghurt is made by fermenting milk. **Yoghurt production** can be affected by different factors.

a) Explain why the **pH** of milk **decreases** as yoghurt is produced.

....

b) For **one** named factor, describe its effect on the rate of yoghurt production.

....

....

Using Enzymes

Q1 The Complacent Cow Company makes **cheese** from cow's milk using an **enzyme** that comes from **genetically modified yeast**. They claim that they "make cheese without cruelty to animals".

a) Name the enzyme that the Complacent Cow Company uses.

....

b) Describe briefly how yeasts can be made to produce this enzyme.

....

c) Suggest why the Complacent Cow Company's cheese might be popular with vegetarians, but cheese from other companies might not be.

....

....

Q2 A sweet manufacturer uses an enzyme produced by **yeast** to convert **sucrose** into **fructose**.

a) Name the enzyme involved in this process.

....

b) Name the **yeast** that naturally produces this enzyme.

....

c) Explain the purpose of converting sucrose into fructose.

....

....

Q3 **Bacteria** produce enzymes to help break down their food. One example is the **protease enzyme**, which breaks down **protein** into amino acids.

Some **washing powders** have the protease added to them. Explain why.

....

....

....

Bac-Wash

Top Tips: Phew — bet you never thought there were so many useful little enzymes out there. Well, there's a shed load, but luckily you only need to know about a couple. Make sure you remember what they are for the exam — it could pick you up some marks, and it'll even impress your mates.

Enzyme Experiments

Q1 Enzymes can be **immobilised** using various methods.

a) Give **one** way that enzymes can be immobilised.

....

b) Suggest **one** benefit of using immobilised enzymes.

....

Q2 Some kinds of **dairy product** are treated to remove the **lactose** (milk sugar).

a) Suggest why this is done.

....

b) Briefly describe how immobilised enzymes are used to produce lactose-free milk.

....

....

c) Suggest how you could test whether the milk produced is definitely lactose-free.

....

....

Q3 **Pectinases** are enzymes that break down pectin in the cell walls of plants. Aslan does an experiment to see how **pectinase** activity varies with **pH**. He adds pectinase to crushed apples at different pH values to release their juice. The graph shows his results.

a) Suggest why the fruit is crushed before pectinase is added.

....

....

Relative pectinase activity

1 2 3 4 5 6 7 8 9 10 11 12 13 14

pH

b) What is the optimum pH for the activity of this pectinase?

....

c) Suggest **one** factor that Aslan needs to keep the same during this experiment.

....

d) Some types of fruit, such as oranges, are more acidic than apples. A different kind of pectinase is needed to get juice from oranges effectively. Suggest how the graph above would be different for a pectinase that works well at extracting juice from oranges.

....

Genetically Modifying Organisms

Q1 Some stages in the production of a **herbicide-resistant maize plant** are listed below. Put the stages in the correct order.

A The herbicide-resistance gene is inserted into *Agrobacterium tumefaciens*.

B Infected cells from maize are grown in a medium containing herbicide.

C The gene that makes a wild corn plant resistant to herbicide is identified.

D *Agrobacterium tumefaciens* is allowed to infect a maize plant.

E The herbicide-resistance gene is cut out from a wild corn plant.

Order: ....

Q2 a) Match the descriptions below to the different stages of **insulin production** by putting the correct letter next to the diagram.

A Insulin produced by the bacteria is purified and can then be used as a treatment.

B The plasmid is put back into the bacteria and they are cultivated until millions of identical bacteria have grown.

C An enzyme cuts the plasmid so that the human section of DNA can be inserted.

D A human DNA sample is taken and a plasmid (bacterial DNA) is removed from the bacteria.

E Enzymes are used to cut the human insulin gene from the human DNA.

1  ....

2 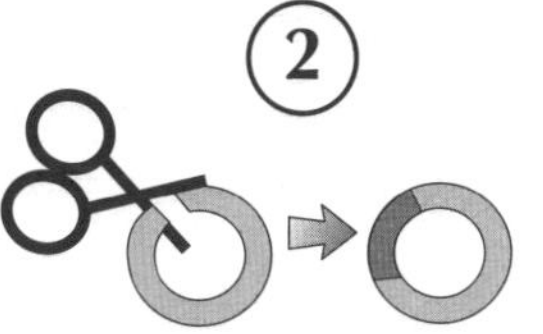 ....

3 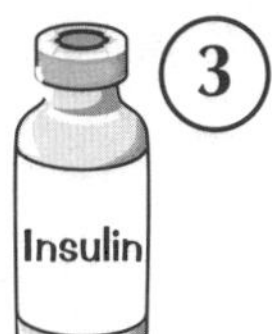

....

4 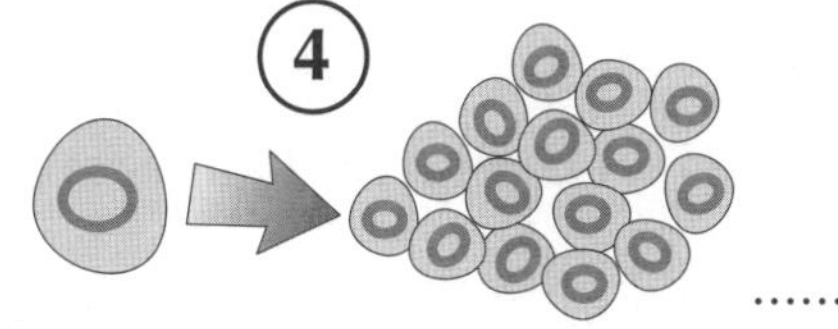 ....

5 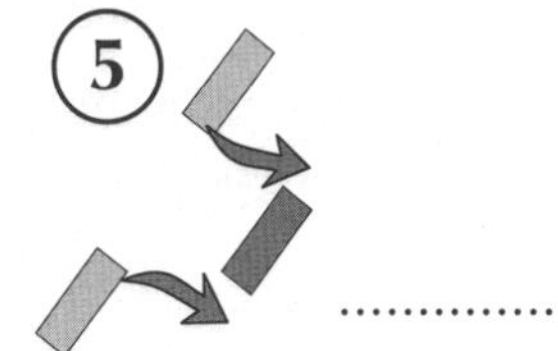 ....

b) Arrange the numbers to give the steps in the correct order. ....

c) i) Describe the role of **restriction enzymes** in the production of insulin.

....

ii) The restriction enzymes leave DNA with 'sticky ends'. What are **sticky ends**?

....

d) Describe the role of **ligase** in insulin production.

....

More on GM Organisms

Q1 Tick the correct box to show whether the statements below are **true** or **false**.

		True	False
a)	Developed countries don't have any health problems.	☐	☐
b)	Tomatoes have been genetically engineered to have 'anti-cancer' properties.	☐	☐
c)	Purple tomatoes have been developed as an easy way to get protein into people's diets.	☐	☐
d)	Flavonoids are molecules that are thought to protect against cancers and heart disease.	☐	☐
e)	Scientists have genetically engineered tomatoes that contain the flavonoid gene.	☐	☐

Q2 a) Use the words provided to fill in the blanks in the passage below.

harmful **kills** **bacterium** **gene** **resistant** **cotton**

Bacillus thuringiensis (Bt) is a .... that can be used in biotechnology. It produces a toxin that .... many of the insect larvae that are .... to crops. The .... for this toxin can be inserted into crops like .... These crops then produce the toxin in their stems and leaves, making them .... to the insect pests.

b) Give **one disadvantage** of using crops that produce Bt toxin rather than normal crops.

....

Q3 Unicourt Biotech, an American company, has developed a new **GM rice** that gives a **higher yield** than ordinary rice and which is also **resistant to diseases**.

Ruritasia is a poor island in South-East Asia. The rice would grow well there, but some of the local farmers **don't** want to use it.

a) Why might it be good for the people of Ruritasia if they used the GM rice?

....

....

b) Some people in Ruritasia object to the use of GM rice. Suggest one objection they might have.

....

c) If the climate in Ruritasia changed, resulting in lack of rain, what kind of GM crop could be used?

....

Feeding More People

Q1 Use the words provided to fill in the blanks in the passage below.

food security	increase	production	rising	nutrition	amount

The world's population is .... very quickly, which means that global food .... must .... too. This is so that we all have enough food to eat with the right balance of .... — this is known as .... We also need to make sure that people still have the same .... of food to eat.

Q2 Some farmers try to reduce the number of **pests** on their crops.

a) Why is it beneficial for farmers to reduce pest numbers?

....

b) Suggest **two** ways in which a farmer can reduce pest numbers.

1. ....

2. ....

Q3 There are two varieties of **wheat plants** that have the characteristics outlined below:

WHEAT PLANT	GRAIN YIELD	RESISTANCE TO BAD WEATHER
Tall plant	High	Low
Dwarf plant	Low	High

a) Describe how selective breeding could be used to create a wheat plant with a **high yield** and **high resistance** to bad weather.

....

....

....

b) Other than selective breeding or managing pests, give **one** way a farmer could increase crop yield.

....

Biofuels

Q1 Tick the box next to the correct definition of **biofuels**.

- Fuels made from plants, animals or their waste products. ☐
- Fuels that have been made through genetic engineering. ☐
- Fuels that are made from animals only. ☐
- Fuels that power biological technologies. ☐

Q2 Overall, **biofuels** don't release as much **carbon dioxide** into the atmosphere as fossil fuels. Explain why this is.

....

....

....

Q3 **Biofuels** are a **renewable** source of fuel and can be used instead of fossil fuels.

a) **i)** Why are biofuels considered to be **renewable**?

....

ii) Give an **advantage** of renewable fuels over fossil fuels.

....

b) One **disadvantage** of using biofuels is that growing the crops needed to make them take up a large amount of land. Explain why this is could be a problem.

....

....

c) Suggest **another disadvantage** of using biofuels.

....

Top Tips: The simple fact is that fossil fuels aren't great for the environment and they're running out — so we need an alternative. Biofuels are pretty handy, but don't be fooled into thinking they're the perfect solution. They've got disadvantages too, so make sure you know the pros AND cons.

Mixed Questions — B3 Topic 3

Q1 Circle the correct word in each pair to complete the sentences below about **food production**.

a) Global food production needs to **increase** / **decrease** so that we all have **food** / **job** security.

b) Crop yield can be improved by genetically engineering plants that are **waterproof** / **resistant** to **pests** / **biogas**.

c) Crop yield can also be improved by selecting and breeding plants with the **best** / **worst** characteristics over several generations, to develop desired **enzymes** / **traits**.

d) Food crops can be **pasteurised** / **genetically engineered** to increase their yield, e.g. by producing **insect-resistant** / **blue-eared** crops.

Q2 The statements below are about **enzymes** that are used in biotechnology. Tick the correct box to show whether each statement is **true** or **false**.

		True	False
a)	Biological washing powders don't contain enzymes.	☐	☐
b)	*Fusarium* is an enzyme that breaks down food.	☐	☐
c)	A bacterium called *Saccharomyces cerevisiae* produces invertase.	☐	☐
d)	Invertase is an enzyme that converts glucose into sucrose.	☐	☐
e)	Chymosin is used in the process of making vegetarian cheese.	☐	☐
f)	You can use immobilised lactase to produce lactose-free milk.	☐	☐
g)	Immobilised enzymes are enzymes that don't work.	☐	☐
h)	Ligase is an enzyme involved in insulin production.	☐	☐

Q3 Charlotte works for a company that uses **microorganisms** to produce their products.

a) How are microorganisms grown on a **large scale**?

....

b) Suggest **one** product that Charlotte's company could manufacture using **bacteria**.

....

c) **i)** Name one other type of microorganism that humans can obtain useful products from.

....

ii) Name **one** product that can be made from the type of microorganism you named in part **i)**.

....

Mixed Questions — B3 Topic 3

Q4 Describe how bacteria are used to make **yoghurt**.

....

....

....

Q5 A company have developed a maize crop that is **frost resistant**. This allows maize to be grown in areas that have previously been too cold for the crop.

a) Describe how the frost-resistance gene is inserted into the maize.

....

....

....

b) Some people are opposed to the genetic modification of plants. Discuss the reasons why.

....

....

....

....

c) Modifying maize in this way is just one application of GM technology. Describe how the following modifications to plants might be an advantage for humans in **developing countries**.

i) Leaves that contain insecticide.

....

ii) Crops with increased nutritional value.

....

Q6 Briefly describe how **mycoprotein** is manufactured.

....

....

....